Stone Breaker

A Driftless Connecticut Series Book

This book is a 2023 selection in the Driftless Connecticut Series, for an outstanding book in any field on a Connecticut topic or written by a Connecticut author.

Alexander Pt.   H.W.Smith

Stone Breaker

The Poet James Gates Percival
and the Beginning of Geology
in New England

KATHLEEN L. HOUSLEY

Wesleyan University Press
Middletown, Connecticut

Wesleyan University Press
Middletown CT 06459
www.wesleyan.edu/wespress

Manufactured in the United States of America
Designed and composed in Chaparral, Anziano, and Calluna type
by Chris Crochetière, BW&A Books, Inc.

A Driftless Connecticut Series Book, funded by the
Beatrice Fox Auerbach Foundation Fund
at the Hartford Foundation for Public Giving

Library of Congress Cataloging-in-Publication Data
available at catalog.loc.gov/
cloth   ISBN 978-0-8195-0028-1
ebook   ISBN 978-0-8195-0029-8

5 4 3 2 1

Frontispiece: Francis Alexander, *James Gates Percival*. Etching
published in *The Poetical Works of James Gates Percival* (1859).

To my grandchildren,
whose early interest in collecting rocks while hiking
has grown into sustained wonder
at the complexity of the natural world

Contents

Color plates appear after page 78

List of Illustrations

[LIST OF ILLUSTRATIONS]

PLATES

Acknowledgments

NOTES ON THE TEXT

I first became interested in James Gates Percival when I taught a course titled *Written in Stone, Painted in Fire* at the Academy of Lifelong Learning at Trinity College; this course was about the influence of geology on nineteenth-century Connecticut Valley poets and artists, among them Emily Dickinson and Frederic Church. I included Percival because he was both a highly regarded poet and a geologist whose greatest achievement was his pioneering work on volcanism and traprock in New England.

I have often explored in my writing what I call the borderlands between science, religion, and the humanities. To me, Percival was the perfect specimen of a dweller in those borderlands where ideas often run counter to those held by the greater world. For instance, as Percival was compiling evidence that the earth was old and traprock was volcanic in origin, he was living in a society that believed the earth was young and had been shaped by Noah's flood. The incongruity Percival faced everyday captured the interest of my Trinity students, in turn spurring me to undertake a full biography. I received encouragement from Robert Thorson, professor and interim Head of Geosciences at the University of Connecticut, whose books on Henry David Thoreau gave me insight into how a person could toggle between poetry and science while living among stolid New Englanders not much interested in either field.

The James Gates Percival papers are in the Yale Collection of American Literature, Beinecke Rare Book and Manuscript Library. Among the papers are many large maps Percival drew of Connecticut, covered with meticulous notations in tiny handwriting. There are also voluminous files of Percival's geological observations, poetry, and translations. I am indebted to the staff at the Beinecke for their willingness to digitize some letters for me when the library was closed due to the Covid epidemic.

The outstanding libraries and knowledgeable staff at Wesleyan University were essential for my research. Copies of Percival's geological report on Connecticut and Charles Upham Shepard's mineralogical report are in the Science Library. Julius Ward's biography of Percival is in Olin Library. Even though they are available online, there is nothing like reading—and holding—the actual books.

The Berlin Historical Society was especially helpful. My thanks to Sallie Caliandri, whose knowledge of the history of Kensington and Berlin is encyclopedic, and to Lorraine Stub and Cathy Nelson, who provided guidance and encouragement. Thanks as well to Heidi Kropf, who gave me a tour of the region, showing me the Percival homestead, Cathole Pass, and other important places. Without their support, this project would have been much more difficult, if not impossible.

I am grateful to Peter LeTourneau, visiting scholar of earth and environmental sciences at Wesleyan University and associate research scientist at the Lamont-Doherty Earth Observatory, Columbia University. My introduction to Peter was via his excellent book *The Traprock Landscapes of New England: Environment, History, and Culture*, with photographs by Robert Pagini, published by Wesleyan University Press. Peter grew up in Meriden in the shadow of the traprock ridges, which impressed on him the power of geology. Peter has been magnanimous in sharing with me both his knowledge and his passion for the traprock ridges, which are under environmental threat. In many ways Peter is Percival's worthy successor. My thanks to Robert Pagini for his superb photographs that provide a sense of continuity between the past and present.

NOTES ON ART

Stone Breaker is illustrated with the paintings of the artist Nelson Augustus Moore, who was a neighbor of Percival's and whose love for the region equaled his. I have included a short biography of Moore in the appendix. However, here in the acknowledgments, I want to thank the people who brought Moore to my attention. I will never forget the moment at the Berlin Historical Society when I inquired whether there were any extant paintings of the region from the time of Percival, and Lorraine Stub fetched a book from the shelves about Nelson Augustus Moore. Opening it was a revelation—there were the traprock ridges as Percival saw them, virtually treeless with farm fields and orchards extending out from the talus slopes, which is not as they appear today. Truly these paintings were a window into the past. Subsequently, several people kindly gave me permission to reproduce Moore's art in this book. Todd and Marenda Stitzer shared their beautiful collection with me. So also did Derik Pulito, who lives on the Percival homestead. Charles Rathbone, Moore's descendent, provided much information and sent me a photo of the Moore family sitting on the porch of the Stone House. Roy Wiseman and Lisa Kugelman gave me permission to use the painting of Percival's home.

The second serendipitous art discovery was John Warner Barber, a contemporary of Percival's who published woodcuts in his book *Connecticut Historical Collections* in 1836. Barber toured the entire state just before Percival began his geological trek. As did Moore, Barber captured how the state looked. While his woodcut technique has sometimes been judged as mediocre, in fact, he was meticulous in getting geological detail correct. My thanks to the Historical Society of Glastonbury for the loan of Barber's *Connecticut Historical Collections*, which served as a visual reference to some of the places Percival visited, including Cotton Hollow in South Glastonbury and Wolf Den in Pomfret.

Finally, thanks to Suzanna Tamminen, director of Wesleyan University Press, who expressed an interest in *Stone Breaker* because of the layering—similar to stratification—of science, poetry, and art into the narrative. "You have crafted a geological study of geology," she wrote. Indeed, that was my goal. Percival would have wanted nothing less.

Introduction

Two rocks sit on my desk. One is a heavy, dark lump of iron slag that I found near the ruins of an eighteenth-century ironworks. It is smooth on one side with a small crater resembling the caldera of a dead volcano. The opposite side is tortuously misshapen with pocks, solidified drips, blobs, and jagged edges—evidence of hot metal splashed onto the ground where it took the shape of whatever it hit. The other rock on my desk is a piece of basalt, also called traprock, which I collected on a hike into the Hanging Hills in Meriden, Connecticut. Columnar in shape, it is gray-brown with a reddish tint. Like the slag, it is very heavy and was formed by immense heat. Unlike the slag, the basalt was once magma that rose up through fissures in the earth's crust. The slag in its present state is no more than 250 years old. The basalt is a staggering 200 million years old.

Nowadays that age comes as no surprise, but in the early nineteenth century the idea that rocks could be millions of years old and the earth itself billions of years old was incomprehensible. The prevailing belief, based on the calculations of a seventeenth-century Irish priest, was that the earth was about six thousand years old. Subsequent to the earth's creation, its surface was reshaped by a worldwide flood, from which deposits settled on the seafloor, where they were compressed into rock. Yet if all rocks came from water, how could volcanoes be explained? Where did igneous rock, derived from the Latin word for fire, originate? These were not idle questions for James Gates Percival, who was born in 1795 in Kensington, Connecticut, in the shadow of the ridges from which my piece of basalt came. "Before the hills in order stood and Earth received her frame," sang parishioners on Sunday mornings, "from everlasting Thou art God to endless years the same." As a boy, Percival certainly knew that well-known hymn by Isaac Watts. Its message was clear: God created the world in an unchanging way as set forth in the first chapter of Genesis. However, to neophyte geologists the rocks themselves sang a contradictory song of an ancient and ever-changing earth where mountains rose up and were worn down; earthquakes caused rivers to dam up and change course; and lava spread across the land, cooling into stone.

Mineralogy and metallurgy were venerable areas of knowledge stretching back to the prehistoric smelting of copper and tin. It was not until the late eighteenth century that geology gained impetus from the canny insights of the Scotsman James Hutton. In fact, Hutton's book *Theory of the Earth; or, an Investigation into the Laws Observable in the Composition, Dissolution, and Restoration of Land upon the Globe* was published the year Percival was born. Hutton's sweeping approach was summarized in the title: there was theory, investigation, and laws that could be derived by means of careful observation, all pertaining to a changing state—not a fixed frame—of composition, dissolution, and restoration that held true throughout the world.[1]

It could be said that geology and James Gates Percival came of age together. And, as with all coming-of-age stories, there was much turmoil for both: geological ideas were denounced from a multitude of pulpits while Percival teetered perilously between genius and mental illness. As he wrote in a poem, he existed in "a middle place between the strong and vigorous intellect a Newton had, and the wild ravings of insanity." Yet from that middle place where brilliance combined with obsession, Percival created a monumental work titled *Report on the Geology of the State of Connecticut*, published in 1842, on which he had spent seven arduous years crisscrossing the entire state on foot at two-mile intervals.

Percival was one of many geologists who began to question the age of the earth. Just as centuries earlier, Galileo and other astronomers had expanded the conception of space, in the process

FIG. I.1. John Warner Barber, *South Eastern View of West Rock and Westville.* Engraving published in *Connecticut Historical Collections*, 1836. When Percival was a student at Yale, he went for long solitary walks to West Rock and East Rock, returning in time to write down the verse he had composed while walking and to review his notes before his first morning class.

demoting the earth from being the center of the solar system to a mere planet orbiting the sun, so geologists had begun to expand the conception of time. Benjamin Silliman, Percival's professor at Yale and lifelong friend, said in a speech in 1843, "Astronomy demands space, geology time." This expansion had major ramifications on how people saw their place in the universe and how they understood their physical world.

Percival's life is worthy of study because it illuminates that subtle shift in perception, which in turn prepared the way for a shift that was even greater. As Percival set out to traverse Connecticut in 1836, Charles Darwin had just returned from his voyage around the world. Publicly, Darwin published in 1839 his *Journal of Re-*

searches into the Geology and Natural History of the Various Countries visited by the H.M.S. Beagle, but privately, he had begun to formulate his theory of natural selection—a theory dependent on geology's stretching out the age of the earth. Although Percival had in his personal library the books of Charles's father, Erasmus Darwin, he did not live to see *On the Origin of Species,* which was published in 1859, three years after his death. Yet for both Darwin and Percival, the process of change was at the center of their research. Percival was not interested in determining the age of a rock but in understanding the enormous cyclical forces that brought the rock to its present state, an idea that Hutton had first put forth.

Percival's main interest was the traprock ridges that stretch in a broken line from north to south, beginning in Massachusetts, crossing Connecticut, and ending at Long Island Sound (see plates 1 and 2). In Massachusetts, the Connecticut River flows through a low point, with Mount Holyoke to the northeast and Mount Tom to the southwest. Then the ridges run relatively straight until they reach the center of Connecticut near Percival's birthplace in Kensington, at which point they dramatically change course, horizontally dividing the Connecticut Valley by stepping eastward in roughly parallel uplifted fault blocks that include West Peak, East Peak, South Mountain, Cathole Peak, Lamentation Mountain, and Chauncey Peak before re-establishing a north-south line at Mount Higby and from there proceeding to the Sound.

In addition to the main ridges, there is a secondary line to the west, which includes such seeming anomalies as Sleeping Giant, in Native American legend the burial site of a giant named Hobbomock, and East Rock and West Rock, which form a dramatic reddish backdrop to New Haven. The Barndoor Hills in Granby, Connecticut, are near the northern terminus of this secondary line. The primary and secondary ridges vary in many ways; some were formed by rising magma that cooled slowly underground (intrusive), while others were formed by lava that buried the Connecticut Valley to great depth and cooled rapidly on the surface (extrusive). It was the difference between the ridges, as exemplified by West Rock (intrusive) in New Haven and the Hanging Hills (extrusive) in Meriden, which stirred Percival's sense of wonder.

One of Percival's insights was that the ridges were not formed during a single geological event but by several events over a vast period of time. He also understood that erosion and sedimentation were ongoing processes of enormous importance. From what he saw on the surface, he constructed mental models of volcanic fissures and their relationship to mountain building. He saw in his mind's eye tilted strata buried underground. It was impossible for Percival to fully understand what was going on, but that did not stop him from prescient hypothesizing.

It wasn't until over a hundred years after Percival's death that the theory of plate tectonics began to take shape, providing an explanation for why traprock rises abruptly in the Connecticut Valley. In brief, the earth's outer crust is composed of movable rigid plates that collide with, pull away from, or grind against each other, powered by forces deep in the mantle. It is at the plate boundaries that earthquakes occur, volcanoes erupt, and mountains are lifted up. By the Mesozoic era, around 251 million years ago, the continents that ride on those plates had converged into a single supercontinent called Pangaea, meaning "all the earth" in Greek. However, the same tectonic forces that led to Pangaea's creation also caused it to split apart around 200–225 million years ago, bringing about the earth's present configuration. As part of the breakup of Pangaea, rift basins, including the Connecticut Valley, were formed along the eastern flank of the Appalachian Mountains, from South Carolina to Maritime Canada and beyond. Then monumental magma plumes upwelled through fissures, either flooding the valley with lava or cooling beneath the surface. Finally, ongoing processes, such as erosion, sedimentation, and tilting, led to the gradual uplift of the traprock, which continues to this day. According to Peter LeTourneau in his book *The Traprock Landscapes of New England*, "The volcanic rocks of the Connecticut Valley are part of one of the largest terrestrial eruptions of basalt in the geologic record—only the extensive lava flows of the Columbia River plateau in the northwestern United States, the Siberian Traps, or India's Deccan Traps are comparable."[2]

In the area where Percival grew up, the ridges are broken by dark defiles, narrow passes, and lakes that look like clear mountain

FIG. I.2. John Warner Barber, *Southern View of the Churches of Meriden*. Engraving with ink wash, published in *Connecticut Historical Collections*, 1836. This view shows the churches, an inn, and a stagecoach while in the background rises the traprock about which Barber wrote, "It is the most prominent object which meets the eye for many miles as you pass either north or south from Meriden."

tarns. From approximately 300 to 1,000 feet in height, the ridges do not compare to the Green Mountains of Vermont or the White Mountains of New Hampshire, where Mount Washington soars to 6,288 feet. What is startling is not the height of the ridges but their abruptness, thrusting up from what was then a gentle pastoral landscape. The ridges are now called the Metacomet Range, but in the eighteenth century they were not recognized as forming a cohesive whole that would warrant the use of the word "range." Generally when people referred to the ridges, they called them simply "the great wall," something that impeded transportation and on which no crops could be grown (see plate 3.) Some sections were given names, such as the Blue Hills and the Hanging Hills, indicative of the way they loom over the landscape as if suspended between earth and sky. Unsurprisingly for a treacherous area with cliffs and talus, some of the ridges became connected with dark legends. Lamentation Mountain was said to have been named for either a lost colonist or an Indian princess who fell to her death.

Between South Mountain and Cathole Mountain, named after a den of panthers, there is a narrow pass with the silhouette of a face jutting from the ledge. Yet for Percival, whose first career was that of a poet, the unseen spirits of the hills were mostly benign. In a long poem titled "Prometheus," he wrote:

> Nature! When looking on thee, I become
> Renewed to my first being, and am pure
> As thou art bright and lovely; from the hum
> Of cities, where men linger and endure
> That wasting death, which kills them with a sure
> But long-felt torture, I now haste away
> To climb thy rugged rocks, and find the cure
> Of all my evils, and again be gay
> In the clear sun, that gilds the fair autumnal day.

Harry Warfel, the editor of the *Uncollected Letters of James Gates Percival*, wrote in his introduction that Percival "was one of America's strangest men of learning. A physician who withdrew early from practice, a botanist, geographer, linguist, and geologist, he was by earliest inclination a poet." During the 1820s, Percival was considered one of the foremost poets in the United States with the talent to challenge the hegemony of British poets such as Byron and Shelley. His poetry was read by future poets, among them Henry David Thoreau and Emily Dickinson, whose family owned an anthology in which his poems appeared. Ralph Waldo Emerson, Edgar Allan Poe, and William Cullen Bryant all read his books. In 1830, John Greenleaf Whittier enthused, "We pity the man who does not love the poetry of Percival." Reprinted in *McGuffey's Reader*, some of his poems were memorized by school children, who stood up and recited, "Again the infant flowers of Spring / Call thee to sport on thy rainbow wing." Unfortunately, Percival's emotional fragility coupled with a sea change in the nature of American poetry assured his fame was short-lived. Warfel claimed that "few other men knew as much as he or could have done the work any better, but he buried his poetic talent and never again recaptured his former verve," turning instead to geology.[3]

The idea that geology was a step down for Percival was also the opinion of the poet James Russell Lowell, who dismissively remarked that Percival had "passed from metrification to petrification." However, from a geological point of view, Percival did not step down at all. Instead, he stepped up in a way that enabled him to break through the constraints of the Biblical conception of time. Curiously, it remains true to this day that geologists consider Percival to have been a towering figure who just so happened to write poetry, while academics in the humanities see him as an all-but-forgotten poet who just so happened to like rocks.[4] There is an implicit bias in the judgment that Percival the *poet* was inherently superior to Percival the *geologist*, who, instead of writing verse, was trying to solve the mystery of how the earth came to be.

Percival was both fully poet and fully geologist, and much more besides. In fact, by the 1830s he was one of the foremost philologists in the nation, versant in more than twenty languages, including Sanskrit and Arabic, and translating numerous works, among them Aeschylus's *Prometheus Bound* from Greek and Goethe's *Faust* from German. When Percival set his mind to something, there was no stopping—no controlling mechanism to shut his mind down.

Thoreau, who was twenty-two years younger than Percival, was a kindred spirit in many ways. A surveyor by trade, he paid close attention to the contours of the land. While his interest in flora and fauna exceeded his interest in geology, Thoreau did not slight the latter, as demonstrated by his essays about the sandy topography of Cape Cod and the rocky summit of Mount Katahdin in Maine. Fortunately, Thoreau was not burdened by severe mental illness, having been blessed with a cheerier disposition and a cooler temper than Percival. Moreover, his family was loving and supportive, whereas Percival's family struggled with depression and alienation. Yet the two men were more alike than not. Both loved to saunter (one of Thoreau's favorite words) across the countryside alone, observing, collecting, and pondering the mysteries of life and the universe. At times this sauntering motivated the penning of a poem, while at other times it resulted in field notes about a particularly favored specimen of a bird's egg or a pebble of rose quartz.

One of Thoreau's friends called him a poet-naturalist. In his book *Walden's Shore*, Robert Thorson, a geologist interested in the scientific aspects of Thoreau's life, explained the dual aspects of his intellect within the framework of systems theory, wherein Thoreau's mind could be classified as an intransitive system with the poetic and the scientific as two equally viable equilibrium states: "During the summer of 1852 he was tottering on the threshold between these two states when he wrote his widely quoted statement that 'every poet has trembled on the verge of science.' The backdrop for this statement was not Thoreau the poet being seduced by science, but Thoreau the scientist being pushed to the brink of poetry." Thorson's explanation also pertains to Percival, who titled one of his autobiographical poems "He Had a Two-fold Nature," one being "the power of thought."[5]

For Percival, geology partially freed him from the necessity of interacting with other humans. Alone on his geological transects, he researched rock formations in his own solitary and scientifically rigorous way, walking miles and miles across the terrain carrying only a hammer and chisel with a specimen bag slung across his shoulder, stopping to examine a granite ledge or to chip out a piece of shale in the hope of finding the fossil of a fish. The earth was solid ground. He could stand on it. He could walk on it. It did not talk back. It did not demand of him social graces he did not possess. It did not question his knowledge or cheat him out of payment for his work.

Were he alive today, James Gates Percival probably would be diagnosed as having an autism spectrum disorder or being a kind of savant. At the very least he would be called a genius. However, those terms either didn't exist in the early nineteenth century or had different meanings. Percival could barely carry on a dialogue with people, yet he could carry on an endless monologue on a vast range of arcane topics, from Serbian poetry to botany, and do so with erudition and in multiple languages. Royal Robbins, a Congregational minister in Kensington and a friend of Percival, wrote, "One peculiarity may be observed in his manner of conversation and that is, when he approaches a subject he enters deeply into it, views it on every side, and pursues it till it is exhausted, if it be exhaustible." Another friend related that if a man interrupted Percival so as to attend to his professional duties but then met him again at a later date, Percival would pick up his monologue exactly where he had left off.[6]

Making everything worse was depression, then commonly called melancholia, which weighed Percival down throughout his life. As a young adult he was suicidal, but by the time he reached middle age the compulsion to kill himself had diminished, although it never went away completely. In Percival's case, melancholia was accompanied by a manic state in which he could not quench his on-fire brain. In addition, there was his paranoia. He often felt misunderstood and unappreciated, attributing nefarious motives to his publishers and co-workers. Yet even the people he perceived as enemies were aware that when he set about a task, such as the geological survey of Connecticut, he did so to a degree normal mortals could not hope to attain. Of course, Percival did not see himself as a normal mortal. It is no surprise that Prometheus was his favorite Greek character because he was the one who stole fire from the gods and gave it to humans, for which act he was chained on a mountaintop where his liver was gouged out each day by birds, only to have it grow back so the torture would be endless.

Many people stepped forward to lend Percival a hand, perceiving him to be a flawed gem—someone who needed to be protected, not shunned. However, Percival was not an easy person to befriend. He tended to bite the hand that fed him, felt slighted over minor things, and had the ability to turn assets into deficits. A story is told that Percival came to hold a grudge against Benjamin Silliman, who had invited him to lecture at a meeting of the Connecticut Academy of Arts and Sciences in New Haven. Percival was supposed to speak for an hour and a half but kept droning on and on, so Silliman, who was presiding, took advantage of a brief pause to rise from his seat and adjourn the meeting, to the utter relief of all the attendees and the anger of Percival.[7]

Yet there was also something about Percival that made people care about him. The best description of him was written by Charles Shepard, who conducted the mineralogical survey that was ancil-

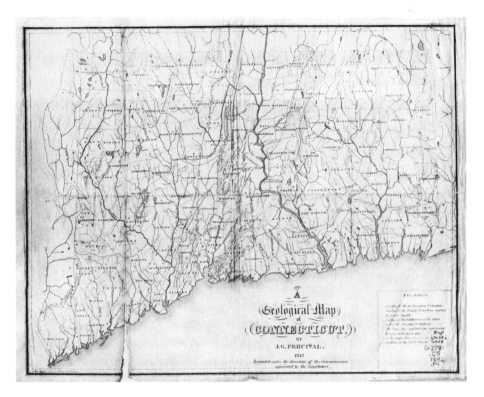

FIG. I.3. J. G. Percival, *Geological Map of Connecticut*, 1842. Published with the *Report on the Geology of the State of Connecticut*, the map accurately showed the uplands, valleys, watercourses, and coastline. The traprock ridges in the center of the state were clearly delineated, including their curvilinear form.

lary to Percival's geological survey and detailed map. A professor at Yale, Shepard spent many months traversing the state with Percival in 1835–36, coming to know him in a personal way. Describing Percival as slender and of medium height with a receding hairline that accentuated his uncommonly expressive eyes, Shepard then turned to his behavior:

> Percival's face, when he was silent, was full of calm, serious meditation; when speaking, it lighted up with thought, and became noticeably expressive. He commonly talked in a mild, unimpassioned undertone, but just above a whisper,

letting his voice sink with rather a pleasing cadence at the completion of each sentence. Even when most animated, he used no gesture except a movement of the first and second fingers of his right hand backward and forward across the palm of his left, meantime following their monotonous unrest with his eyes, and rarely meeting the gaze of his interlocutor. He would stand for hours when talking, his right elbow on a mantel-piece, if there was one near, his fingers going through their strange palmistry; and in this manner, never once stirring from his position, he would not infrequently protract his discourse till long past midnight. An inexhaustible, undemonstrative, noiseless, passionless man, scarcely evident to you by physical qualities, and impressing you, for the most part, as a creature of pure intellect.[8]

There is only one biography of Percival, *The Life and Letters of James Gates Percival*. Published in 1866, it was written by Julius H. Ward, who had been deeply impressed by Percival's poetry as an undergraduate at Yale. Although he had never had the opportunity to meet him, Ward did the best he could, compiling the voluminous papers that the executor of Percival's estate had presented to him, supplementing them with remembrances he solicited from many of Percival's acquaintances and family. There was a component of desperation about Ward's efforts for two reasons. First, he was a minister with little free time to devote to the project, which, he said, "made my progress slow and discouraging." Second, he had possession of a draft of a biography written by Erasmus D. North, MD, a professor of elocution at Yale and a friend of Percival, who had died before completing it. When Ward's book was published, it was criticized as being a loose collection of items rather than an actual biography, a criticism with which Ward would have readily agreed, having written in the preface, "Indeed, my work has been mainly and chiefly the editing of the poet's own letters and papers, and the reminiscences of those who knew him intimately." Fortunately, it is as a collection that the book is of value.[9]

Most of the essays on Percival written since the publication of *The Life and Letters of James Gates Percival* draw heavily from the numerous stories about his strange behavior. Yet those stories present a problem to a biographer because they can take on mythic proportions that overwhelm the facts. Only by looking at Percival as a geologist does a fuller and more nuanced picture of an enormously complex man appear.

It would be an error to see Percival solely as an objective scientist determined to discover the secrets of traprock. The geological survey of Connecticut was commissioned in 1835 by the state legislature for purely economic reasons. In 1830, the first railroad in the United States had been built in Baltimore, Maryland, and suddenly iron was in huge demand for trains and tracks. In fact, in the history of the world there had never been such a demand for metals. Fortunes could be made but only if ore could be found. From 1835 to his death in 1856 in Wisconsin, where he had gone first to assess lead mines and then to conduct a state survey as he had done in Connecticut, Percival's worth as an asset to the national economy rose steadily because as a geologist he knew how to locate ore.

Percival never lost his love of poetry and languages, publishing his last collection, *The Dream of a Day*, in 1843, one year after the Connecticut survey was published. To Percival, the irreconcilable aspects of his personality were reconcilable, indeed, complementary. In the title poem, an affirming voice speaks to Percival, "Nerved to a stern resolve, fulfill thy lot / Reveal the secrets nature has unveiled thee."

Percival's last years in Wisconsin were productive and happy, contrary to what might be expected. His behavior was still strange, but he was better able to deal socially with the miners and settlers he met. They, in turn, accepted him as he was—a kind of wonder of nature. When, at the end of his life, the children in Hazel Green, Wisconsin, called him the Old Stone Breaker, it was as close as he would come to a nickname bestowed with affection. It was also the right one.

Stone Breaker

FIG. 1.1. Edwin Percival, *Portrait of James Gates Percival*. Oil on canvas. James Gates Percival Collection, Yale Collection of American Literature, Beinecke Rare Book and Manuscript Library. Talented but mentally unstable, Edwin Percival painted this portrait of his brother probably no later than 1820. It is a gentler depiction than some of the other portraits of Percival in which he is portrayed as dramatically intense (see frontispiece).

ONE

A Tranquil and Tumultuous Childhood

James Gates Percival was born on September 15, 1795, in Kensington, Connecticut, the third child of Elizabeth Hart and Dr. James Percival. Harriet was born in 1790, Edwin in 1793, then James, and finally Oswin in 1797.[1] It was a peaceful time: twelve years after the end of the Revolutionary War, when George Washington was serving his second term as president. It was a peaceful place: the farmland to the east of the traprock ridge. The wood-frame house with a center chimney stood on a hill close to the road (now named Percival Avenue). Nearby, the meandering Mattabesett River powered several waterwheels as it flowed from its source up in the traprock. To the east was Great Swamp, which lent its name to the first church parish—the Great Swamp Society.

In a poem titled "The Dream of a Day," written many years later, Percival recalled being blissfully alone in the pastures and orchards near his home, listening intently to summer: close at hand were the sounds of the "drone bee's hum" and "the stir of the insect swarms"; in the middle distance were the sounds of "the clacking wheat in a cornfield, at the mill the circling 'plash" while from the mountainside came the faint echo of bleating sheep and lowing cows. In another poem titled simply "Home," he wrote, "I leave the world of noise and show to wander by my native brook; / I ask in life's unruffled flow no treasure but my friend and book." Long after he had grown up and moved away, his memories of Kensington provided solace. Bubbling streams sparkling with sunlight, hidden glades, moss-covered rocks, and sharp craggy cliffs appeared again and again in his poetry—the "paradise" of his heart and the "favorite contemplation" of his mind.[2]

Kensington may have been pastoral but it was not a backwater, one of the reasons being the nearby Berlin Turnpike that threaded its way between the traprock ridges to connect the twin state capitals of New Haven (to the south on Long Island Sound) and Hartford (to the north on the banks of the Connecticut River). Only thirty-four miles apart as the crow flies, both cities could be reached by stagecoach that traveled up and down the turnpike on a regular basis carrying not only passengers but also the most recent newspapers, gazettes, and books. The turnpike's route makes clear that the longstanding rivalry between the two cities had a geologic component because the traprock ridges were a hindrance to commerce (see plate 4). So also was the abrupt change in direction of the Connecticut River, which cut its way out of the central valley near Middletown. The result was that Hartford benefited from lucrative river trade while New Haven did not. Connecticut was known as "the land of steady habits." Although that phrase referred only to its stolid people, somehow the earth itself was supposed to share the same attributes of utilitarian conformity and fair play. Even as a boy in Kensington, Percival was aware that this was not so. All he had to do was to walk out his front door to realize the impact of geology on commerce and culture: to the west— the great wall; to the south—Cathole Mountain and the Hanging Hills; to the southeast—Mount Lamentation.[3]

Most of the anecdotal information about Percival's childhood comes from Julius Ward's biography, in which Percival is characterized as intellectually precocious but shy and withdrawn, living mostly in his own world (see plate 5). Ward indicated, without providing any corroborating evidence, that Percival's mother, Elizabeth Hart (called Betsy), was emotionally unstable. Born in Kensington in 1769, Elizabeth was the daughter of Matthew Hart and Elizabeth Hopkins. "She had a sensitive, nervous temperament, and was inclined at times to melancholy; but her mind was strong and keen and clear; and she added to her native gifts a better education than women usually had in those days; she had a good literary taste, and in later years heartily appreciated the poetical reputation of her son. Her volumes of his poetry are thoroughly worn from frequent use." Samuel Griswold Goodrich, who came to know Percival when he was a young man, wrote that Elizabeth Hart had a "susceptible and delicate organization, with a tendency to excessive mental development."[4]

"Excessive mental development" apparently ran in the female side of the family because Elizabeth's relative Emma Hart was destined to become one of the foremost female educators in the country, establishing the renowned Troy Female Seminary in 1820 with her husband John Willard. Emma's father was a farmer and a free thinker in Kensington who encouraged all his daughters to learn geometry and philosophy and to participate in intellectual discussions with the male members of the family. It seems that Elizabeth's father, Matthew Hart, also took a liberal approach to educating females. According to Ward, Elizabeth had a strong influence on her children.[5]

Percival's precociousness was obvious from the start. There is a story about his borrowing a book on astronomy from the schoolmaster in Kensington. He was just beginning to read and the book seemed beyond his ability. Undaunted, he set to work over the weekend sounding out every word. By Monday, to the amazement of the schoolmaster, he could read the first chapter without hesitation. Horatio Gridley, a friend of the family, remembered that Percival was the best speller in the class, marching to the head of the spelling line time and again, but he never played games with the other children. "He was remarkably quiet and inoffensive," Gridley said. "He used to stay in the school-room at noon, when the other boys were at play, and would sometimes complain if they made too much noise. He seldom went out at recess."[6]

As is the case with many prodigies, Percival educated himself by voluminous reading, beginning with his father's excellent library and continuing with the library that belonged to the nearby Congregational church, which functioned as a center of learning as well as worship. Royal Robbins, the minister, wrote, "At this period he lived in a world of his own, an ideal world. He knew and he cared very little respecting the real world of mankind. His cast of mind was highly imaginative; and, aided by his extensive recollections of history, geography, and other readings, he lived and acted very much according to the fancies which his knowledge enabled him to contrive." Robbins's recollection was later corroborated by Percival himself, who wrote in a poem that his boyhood reading led to fantasies about ascending the pyramids, riding an Arab steed across the desert, and roaming the plains of central Asia "where the savage Hun and Mogol in devouring torrents rushed."[7]

Because of the numerous books written during this period, a child could indeed roam the world while staying at home. As a young teenager, Percival kept an alphabetical list of 107 books he had read, among them Adam Smith's seminal work on economics *The Wealth of Nations*, William Fordyce Mavor's multivolume *Universal History*, and Oliver Goldsmith's *Natural History*, which had beautiful engravings of plants and animals.[8] Among his geography books was the monumental two-volume work by Jedidiah Morse, a Yale graduate. Its full title was *The American Universal Geography; or, a View of the Present State of the Empires, Kingdoms, States, and Republics in the Known World and of the United States of America in Particular in Two Parts*, but it was commonly known by its abbreviated title, *Universal Geography*. Morse's interest in geography stemmed in part from a strong sense of patriotism fueled by a desire to edify American citizens who had been subservient to Great Britain but who were now citizens of a free and independent republic. For Percival, *Universal Geography* (with its mixture of astronomy, geology, history, and culture) was heady stuff that helped to set the direction of his life. Charles Shepard, who worked with him on the Connecticut geological survey during the 1830s, noted that as an adult Percival was as familiar with the geography and geology of England as he was of New England even though he had never been to England. Shepard believed that it was Percival's reading of *Universal Geography* as a child that "determined his taste for those geographical studies in which he subsequently was distinguished."[9]

Despite Robbins's observation that Percival did not care about the real world, Percival's juvenilia reveal he followed the news of the day closely. For instance, he expressed in a poem his opposition to slavery, calling on the citizens of New England to cease "that horrid trade which grows in human blood," and he voiced his disapproval of the 1807 Embargo Act that President Thomas Jefferson had imposed on England. These were serious topics for a child to address, particularly in rhymed verse.[10]

Percival also followed what was happening in natural history and natural philosophy, which at the time were peculiar mixtures of observation, classification, enlightenment, romanticism, indigestible chunks of religion, and even patriotism. The following example sums up all those elements and sheds light on how Percival first learned to conceive of science, which even at this early date was at the beck and call of politics and commerce. In 1801, a farmer discovered huge bones in a bog in Newburgh, New York, near the Hudson River. Charles Willson Peale, a natural historian and artist best known for his painting of George Washington, purchased the muddy site from the farmer and oversaw the dig, even designing bailing equipment with pulleys and buckets to remove the water. Once the bones were exhumed, Peale transported them (along with those found in two nearby sites) to Philadelphia, where he planned to display them to the public in his natural history museum alongside his substantial collection of stuffed birds, animals, and other specimens. Like a cabinet of curiosities taken up a scientific notch, Peale's museum was carefully categorized according to the taxonomy of Carl Linnaeus, the eighteenth-century Swedish naturalist who had formulated the concept of three kingdoms—animal, vegetable, and mineral—divided into class, order, family, genus, and species, thereby providing a framework to understand the natural world.[11]

It took Peale's slave, Moses Williams, several months to put the bones of the mastodon together by trial and error, drawing on his knowledge of the African elephant, before Peale threw open the museum doors to the public. With dramatic flair, he hosted dinner parties for carefully selected luminaries, placing the banquet table beneath the ribcage of the beast. Bones and teeth of mastodons had been discovered elsewhere, but this was the first time in the United States that people were able to view an entire skeleton. Some people insisted that the bones of this *Incognitum*, as Thomas Jefferson called it, came from an elephant and were no more than six thousand years old, the presumed age of the earth. Other people, with a more skeptical mindset, were not so sure. Perhaps they were the bones of an extinct species, although according to the Bible no species ever went extinct but were kept alive, two by two, on the ark, repopulating the earth "after their own kind" when the flood waters receded. That raised another tantalizing idea: perhaps the creature was not extinct but was roaming the unexplored west. When in 1804, three years after the discovery of the bones, Thomas Jefferson sent out the Corps of Discovery under the leadership of Meriwether Lewis and William Clark to find a trade route to the Pacific, he hoped they might also discover grazing placidly on prairie grass the *Incognitum*.

The story of the mastodon was a sensation and was covered in newspapers up and down the eastern seaboard, supposedly proving that the new world was not the degenerate stepchild of the old world, as some European scientists had derisively claimed—a claim that wounded the pride of Jefferson and Peale. Now with its very own mastodon, the United States stood tusk and ribcage above Europe. Even in bucolic Kensington, the imagination of the citizenry was stirred. During that period, when a farmer turned over his fields in the spring, he kept one eye on the plow to keep the rows straight and the other eye cocked for big bones jutting up through the loam. Eventually bones were found in the region (about which Percival reported in his *Geology of the State of Connecticut*), but at the time no bones were unearthed in Kensington—excepting those of one dead goose. According to his brother Oswin, James found the carcass in a field near the house. As carefully as he could, he gathered up the bones, brought them home, and then numbered and labeled each one for display.[12] It is not known when he learned taxonomy. However, as a young man he wrote a poem praising Linnaeus, whom he described as an ancient priest bringing light into nature's darkness, revealing that knowledge of God was "given to those whose hearts can feel him in the flowers."[13]

Likewise, Percival showed a passion for mineralogy, collecting from brooks "curious stones and diamond-shaped crystals."[14] These, too, were identified and labeled, a habit that became lifelong, culminating in the eight thousand specimens Percival collected while surveying Connecticut in the 1830s. In the damp sand bordering the brooks, he drew maps of the kingdoms and places about which he had read, using pebbles to mark boundaries and the locations of cities, writing in a poem that in the summertime he would "rear an empire" on the shores (see plate 6). "There cities rose and palaces and towers caught the first light of morning," he wrote. "There the fleet lent all its snowy canvas to the wind and bore with awful front against the foe."[15]

Percival's affinity for poetry revealed itself early. He read the works of the Scottish poet James Thomson, the British poet Robert Bloomfield, and the American poet Joel Barlow, among others. Their poems were very popular and were commonly found in the libraries of educated families as well as in private lending libraries. Paying homage to Thomson's *The Seasons*, Percival named his first book of poems *The Seasons of New England*. He also emulated Bloomfield, who wrote in *The Farmer's Boy* about the quotidian details of farm life, such as feeding turnips to cattle on a winter day. Percival's version was about a boy who feeds Indian corn to the lowing ox and patient cow as a winter storm approaches. In contrast to Bloomfield and Thomson, Joel Barlow was a Connecticut native, Yale graduate, diplomat, and political gadfly. Barlow's claim to poetic fame was first published in 1787 as *Vision of Columbus*, which he revised significantly over a twenty-year period, increasing its length from 4,700 lines to 8,350 lines and changing its title to *The Columbiad*. The poem took the form of a tendentious dialogue between Christopher Columbus and an angel in which all of history culminated in George Washington's triumph over England in the Revolutionary War. Percival mimicked Barlow in his mock-heroic poem "Commerciad," in which he declared that Barlow "shines the Homer of our age, Genius and Elegance adorn the page."[16]

Until Percival was eleven years old, his father provided a steadying hand, attempting to coax him out of his "morbid shyness and shrinking sensitiveness." Ward described Dr. James Percival as having a strong constitution and a vigorous mind. "He easily grasped a subject, and was noted for keeping his own counsel and doing things entirely in his own way." He was well-read, prosperous, and respected as a physician, but he had an independent streak about religion, being a Freemason. While Freemasons were not atheists, neither were they considered orthodox Christians, which made them slightly suspect in New England. Ward considered the family to be moral but not distinctly religious. However, what Percival remembered most about his father was his skill as a physician who "eased the raking pain" and "cooled the fever's racking glow," returning people to health.[17]

In light of the terrible disease that was about to ravage the Percival family, it is worthwhile to take a brief look at the nature of medicine at the beginning of the nineteenth century. Only a few colleges offered courses in medicine, Harvard and the University of Pennsylvania among them.[18] If a young man expressed an interest in medicine, he became apprenticed to a doctor in the same way that an aspiring lawyer "read" law under the tutelage of a lawyer. During his apprenticeship, he did not learn about disease causation and prevention because no one knew about germs. Vaccination using cowpox to prevent smallpox was a common practice, but no one understood how it worked. Sickness was thought to be caused by bad air (miasma), bad blood, or an energy imbalance (known as "the principal of excitability"), which could be corrected by either purging or bloodletting. Few medicines were available and some of those that were thought to be safe and effective were actually poisonous, among them calomel—a form of mercury. Without knowledge of disease causation, physicians put everyone at risk, including themselves, by spreading germs via dirty hands, clothes, and coughing.

In the winter of 1806–7, what was thought to be a typhus epidemic broke out in Kensington and the surrounding towns (see plate 7). Traveling by sleigh in early December, Dr. Percival attended several sick people, fell ill himself, and spread the disease to his wife and four children. By the time the epidemic abated, Dr. Percival and seventeen-year-old Harriet were dead, and the others were so critically ill it took them many months to recover. Dr. Horatio Gridley, a physician in Berlin who knew the Percival family well, gave the following harrowing description of the progression of the disease. While visiting a grievously ill family in Worthington (now part of Berlin), Dr. Percival showed the first strange signs. "He fell asleep while sitting by the fire and manifested an aberration of mind." He then returned home and took an emetic in the afternoon in an effort to purge himself of the impurity or imbalance that had seized him, but it did not help:

> The next morning he sat at table, and took some tea in his mouth which he spitted out, and shed tears. He arose and examined his tongue by the glass. Disease shortly confined him to his house, and derangement became permanent during the latter part of the disease. He died January 21, 1807, at the age of forty. His daughter died of the same disease nineteen days after her father. She had a protracted illness of fifty-two days. Edwin was taken sick the night his father died; James was taken the night after his father was buried; and his wife, a week before his daughter died. These all recovered after a long confinement. It will be seen that the mother and three of her four children were sick at the same time. Dr. Percival came down to the grave in the fullness of life in the midst of his usefulness. His loss was deeply and extensively felt.[19]

At that time, the name typhus was a catchphrase used for a wide range of diseases that were febrile in nature and often accompanied by a rash. Given the lack of understanding of disease causation, typhoid and typhus were often confused. However, the symptoms in this case align with neither. Instead, they align with a third disease, called New England spotted fever, which went by the medical name typhus syncopalis. An epidemic occurred in the middle part of the state in 1807 to 1809, exactly the period of time in which Dr. Percival became ill. Another epidemic occurred about fifteen years later in the same area. A recent analysis has revealed that typhus syncopalis was most likely meningitis (unknown at that time), which helps explain Dr. Percival's lethargy and mental derangement.[20] The key to the diagnosis of meningitis came from a paper written by Dr. Thomas Miner about an epidemic in 1823 in Middletown, which is near Kensington. Dismayed by the hundreds of critically ill patients in his care, Miner gave a detailed description of the epidemic, which he was convinced was a disease of the brain and nervous system. The initial symptoms were headache, dizziness, and extreme exhaustion followed by restlessness, delirium, nausea, skin lesions, stiff neck, and paralysis. Miner described the afflicted as looking like they had suffered a concussion or stroke.[21]

Unfortunately, meningitis can cause permanent damage to survivors. It is possible that the mental illness that afflicted all three of the surviving siblings in the Percival family was caused or exacerbated by the disease. The descriptions of James prior to the epidemic are of a prodigy who was slightly withdrawn but not mentally ill. The descriptions of him as a teenager after the epidemic indicate serious problems. Samuel Griswold Goodrich wrote in his *Recollections of a Lifetime* that when Percival was a Yale student, he frequently visited the Goodrich house in Berlin, where he was "subject to paroxysms of great depression of spirits" to the point of contemplating suicide.[22] As an adult, Edwin was also suicidal, ultimately starving himself to death, and Oswin spent the last years of his life in an insane asylum, having been declared incompetent to handle his own affairs.[23] At the very least the disease damaged James's vocal cords so that he spoke softly, almost in a whisper. He was also exquisitely sensitive to touch, telling people he felt as if he were made of glass and would shatter if someone touched him.[24] It was not just the grief that would stay with him but the terror. For the rest of his life, Percival was death-haunted.

In a poem titled "Night Watching," Percival wrote of a woman sitting beside a dying man. While the scene is imagined, there are elements of it that could only have arisen from memory. Outside, the moon shines serenely, but inside, its light only serves to make more drear "the dark of pestilence" as the woman rests her hand on the man's "clay-cold forehead." Unable to speak, he drifts away from all sight and sound while she draws "contagion from the lips that were to her still beautiful as roses, though so pale, they seemed like a thin snow-curl." The poem ends in devastating silence:

The homes of men
Were now all desolate, and darkness there,
And solitude and silence took their seat
In the deserted streets, as if the wing
Of a destroying angel had gone by
And blasted all existence, and had changed
The gay, the busy, and the crowded mart
To one cold, speechless city of the dead.[25]

The catastrophe led to the breakup of the family because when they had recovered, James, then about thirteen, and Edwin were sent away by their mother to a boarding school run by their uncle on Long Island, which turned out to be a miserable experience. In a long poem titled "The Suicide," written between 1815 and 1820, James wrote: "Abused, neglected, fatherless, no hand / To guide or guard him, left alone to steer / His dangerous way—can youth securely stand / When not a parent, friend, or hope is near?"[26]

When Percival entered Yale in 1810 at the age of fifteen, he was emotionally unstable. He was nicknamed "the poet" by the other students, an appellation that should have been taken as a compliment but that he construed as ridicule. With a vaunted opinion of his abilities, in his freshman year he gave a collection of his poetry (probably *Seasons of New England*) to Noah Webster, hoping to get his support for its publication. In light of Percival's age and the fact that the poetry was derivative, Webster advised him to wait. The same advice was given to him by Hezekiah Howe, who was an influential bookseller in New Haven. Word spread among the students of Percival's presumptuousness in thinking his poetry good enough to be published. According to his freshman roommate, Nathaniel S. Wheaton, "he burst into a passionate flood of tears, and sobbed out, 'I don't care, I will be a poet.'" Wheaton wrote, "after that we were careful how we touched the tender spot." Nevertheless, Percival had had enough of Yale; he threw down his books mid-semester and stomped back to Kensington to live with his mother (who had remarried) and to work on the farm (see plate 8). Later he reconsidered his decision and returned to Yale, grabbing a ride on a wagon filled with apples that his brother was taking to the market in New Haven. From then on, he continued to write poetry but did not seek public affirmation. Instead, he posted poems anonymously around campus, getting into trouble only once, when he scribbled a poem on one of the columns of the chapel.[27] However, Percival was aware of the terrifying polarity in his mind, describing himself as follows in a poem titled "Pleasures of Childhood":

> There is a middle place between the strong
> And vigorous intellect a Newton had,
> And the wild ravings of insanity;
> Where fancy sparkles with unwearied light,
> Where memory's scope is boundless, and the fire
> Of passion kindles to a wasting flame,
> But will is weak, and judgment void of power,
> Such was the place I held, the brighter part
> Shone out, and caught the wonder of the great
> In tender childhood, while the weaker half
> Had all the feebleness of infancy.[28]

What Yale offered Percival was entry into the world of science. And the man who would open the door to that world was Benjamin Silliman, Yale's first professor of the natural sciences.

TWO

Benjamin Silliman Brings Science to Yale

In a portrait of Benjamin Silliman painted in 1825, the traprock columns of West Rock rise up in the background into a sky filled with billowing clouds (see plate 9). A dramatic red curtain with dark shadows curves diagonally across the middle ground, giving the impression that it is being drawn aside to reveal what was once hidden. In the foreground stands Silliman, tall, handsome, self-assured, dressed in a black coat and a white shirt. He holds a quartz crystal in his right hand while on a marble table in front of him are rocks and a gold pocket watch with a jeweled fob underscoring the role of time in geology. His left hand rests on a lectern covered in notes curling up at the corners as if much used. Silliman is nearing the midpoint of his career at Yale, which began with his graduation in 1796 followed by his appointment as a tutor in 1799. His career would end in 1855—fifty-nine years in which he would teach thousands of students, Percival among them. He would reach thousands more through the pages of *The American Journal of Science and Arts* (now the *American Journal of Science*), the oldest continuously running publication of its kind in the United States, which he established in 1818. It is not possible to understand Percival's life as a geologist without first understanding Silliman and the ideas about the history of the earth that he instilled in all his students.[1]

The portrait of Silliman conveys the sense of fulfilled promise, yet at the beginning of his career that promise lacked direction. First, Silliman trained as a lawyer and was admitted to the

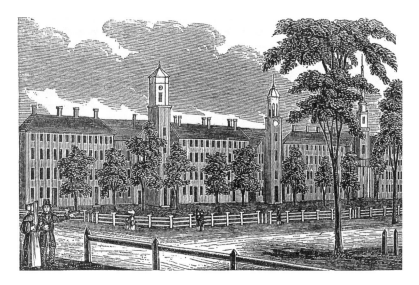

FIG. 2.1. John Warner Barber, *Yale College*. Engraving published in *Connecticut Historical Collections*, 1836. Benjamin Silliman delivered his first chemistry lecture at Yale in 1804. By the time he retired in 1855, he had taught thousands of students including Percival who hoped to follow in his footsteps as a professor. To Percival's regret, he was not offered the position because of a speech impediment that affected his ability to lecture.

bar only to realize he disliked law. Then he was appointed as a tutor at Yale, which required him to help students prepare for recitations. One student under his charge recalled that Silliman was not always up to the task: "Benny blushed as he tried to help—foundering in the mire of a problem which he was unprepared to solve."[2]

Fortunately for Silliman, Yale had a problem to which he turned out to be the answer. The curriculum was crammed with rhetoric, Hebrew, Greek, ecclesiastical history, classical studies, and theology, all intended to shape the minds of future ministers. Natural history and chemistry were not considered important. In *Benjamin Silliman: A Life in the Young Republic*, Chandos Brown writes that when Silliman was a student at Yale, scientific apparatus was sparse and decrepit. There was no laboratory, chemicals, or glassware for experiments. The orrery was rusty and its orbs representing the sun, moon, and planets were stuck in place. The four-foot telescope was covered with dust and could not be turned.[3] However, times were changing and Yale needed to keep up.

To offer courses in natural history, Timothy Dwight, president of Yale, decided to hire someone knowledgeable, but there were very few men in the United States who met that requirement. John Maclean was at the College of New Jersey in Princeton. A graduate of the University of Glasgow, he was up-to-date on the latest advances in chemistry in Europe. James Woodhouse was at the University of Pennsylvania, having added to his undergraduate education by visiting scientists in England. There was no one at Harvard, which was in the same woeful position as Yale—heavy on theology and light on everything else. Without a single prospect, Dwight decided to select an intelligent young man and pay him to study, if need be in Europe, and then to return to Yale as a professor. Dwight asked Silliman, then twenty-four years old, to take on the task. He was the logical choice because he had already attempted to lecture on chemistry even though his knowledge was rudimentary. He had gone so far as to write to Maclean inquiring about what texts he should obtain. However, Silliman was cognizant of the fact that chemistry could not be learned by means of books alone; hands-on experiments were essential, but none of the books that Maclean suggested showed how to conduct them. Aware of his own shortcomings, Silliman readily accepted Dwight's offer. In his reminiscences written at the end of his life, Silliman explained why: "I kept [available chemistry texts] secluded in my secretary, occasionally reading in them privately. This reading did not profit me much. Some general principles were intelligible, but it became at once obvious to me that to see and perform experiments and become familiar with many substances was indispensable to any progress in Chemistry and of course I must resort to Philadelphia which presented more advantages in science than any other place in our country."[4]

In 1802, Silliman went to the University of Pennsylvania in Philadelphia to attend the chemistry lectures of Woodhouse, who had just returned from England, bringing back from the laboratory of Humphry Davy a galvanic battery to use in his lectures.

"The chemical lectures were important to me, who had as yet seen few chemical experiments," Silliman wrote. "Those performed by Dr. Woodhouse were valuable, because every fact, with its proof, was an acquisition to me. The apparatus was humble, but it answered to exhibit some of the most important facts in the science, and our instructor delighted in the performance of experiments. He had no proper assistant, and the work was imperfectly done but still it was a treasure to me."[5]

Despite the praise, Silliman was highly critical of Woodhouse for not making explicit connections in his lectures between chemistry and the creative power of God as seen in his handiwork. In lecturing on the 1793 yellow fever epidemic that had killed approximately five thousand people in Philadelphia, Woodhouse had, according to Silliman, "treated with levity and ridicule the idea that the visitations of the yellow fever might be visitations of God for the sins of the people."[6] Woodhouse's claim that the epidemic was due solely to physical causes was sacrilege to Silliman, who believed that it was a sign of God's righteous anger. Silliman was also appalled when a professor of botany suggested that the students visit Charles Willson Peale's museum to view his collection of plants—on a Sunday. Puritanism was dead in Philadelphia. It was alive and well in New Haven, where religious awakenings were commonplace, periodically sweeping Yale students into paroxysms of devotion and sometimes despair. Silliman himself had been required to declare his faith in order to be hired as a tutor.[7]

Because President Dwight hoped to start a medical school at Yale, he had directed Silliman to attend the lectures of Benjamin Rush, considered the foremost physician in the nation, and Casper Wistar, a highly respected anatomist. Both men had received their doctorates from the University of Edinburgh in Scotland. Unfortunately, Silliman was no more at ease with Rush than he was with Woodhouse. In his introductory medical lecture, Rush had told Silliman that the lancet was the "magnum donum Dei,"—the major gift of God. Silliman dropped his course. Silliman found Wistar, whose family was Quaker, more to his liking because he included in his anatomy lectures the connection to heavenly design. A sociable man who regularly opened his home during the winter to students and friends for intellectual discussion, Wistar helped Silliman enjoy his time in Philadelphia, introducing him to important people, including Robert Hare, a wealthy member of the Chemical Society of Philadelphia who had his own private laboratory. One of Hare's most useful contributions was a compound blowpipe, which became a standard item in chemical laboratories. Through Wistar, Silliman also met Joseph Priestley, the famous British discoverer of oxygen, who had come to the United States under duress because of his support for the ideals of the French Revolution.[8]

In 1803, Silliman traveled to Princeton to visit Maclean, observing his method of teaching and learning the proper way to set up a college laboratory. Besides having been educated in Edinburgh, Maclean had spent time in Paris studying Lavoisier's revolutionary work in chemistry. As a result, he brought to the United States the most advanced chemical ideas and techniques then available. Not connected to a medical school, Maclean's laboratory was the first of its kind dedicated solely to chemistry. Years later Silliman wrote that it was Maclean, not the professors at the University of Pennsylvania, who influenced him the most: "I regard him as my earliest master of Chemistry, and Princeton as my first starting point in that pursuit."[9]

While Silliman was studying in Philadelphia, a new building (titled simply the Lyceum) was under construction at Yale that was to contain the chemistry laboratory. Silliman was shocked to discover on his return that the laboratory was located in the cellar and was nothing like Maclean's laboratory at Princeton. Only reachable by ladder, the laboratory was "a gloomy cavern, fifteen or sixteen feet below the surface of the ground into which . . . little more light glimmered than just enough to make the darkness visible." It seemed a place more appropriate for medieval alchemy than for modern chemistry. Silliman lost no time in asking the leadership at Yale to come for a visit. They were as aghast as he was and subsequently approved the digging of a trench around the outside of the new building to let in light. That helped a little, but the room was still too damp to conduct experiments. So Silliman set to work and had paving stones laid and a new entry constructed so that students did not have to descend a ladder. He also ordered pipes to be installed to bring in water from a nearby well. Then he set up tables for glassware and apparatus.[10]

Silliman delivered his first official chemistry lecture at Yale on April 4, 1804.[11] Because natural history was so broad, Silliman knew he needed more education in chemistry and mineralogy as well as more laboratory equipment. So in 1805, he packed his trunks and boarded the *Ontario* sailing to England, landing in Liverpool a month later. With a grant of $10,000, he had been directed by Dwight to buy scientific apparatus, mineral specimen collections, books, and whatever was necessary to establish natural history firmly at Yale. Silliman did not let Dwight down.

At the time Silliman left for England, he believed (as did most people in Europe and the United States) that the earth was about six thousand years old. James Ussher (1581–1656), an Irish bishop, had calculated the age using Biblical and historical events. The date of creation was precise—October 22, 4004 BC, in the evening, making October 23 the first full day.[12] That there was an actual start date proved that the world was ordered and everything was in its rightful place. This is what Percival as a boy was taught in church and school in Kensington, and eventually in Silliman's classroom at Yale. Furthermore, the number six thousand was countable; it could be grasped. This mattered because when geologists began to stretch the age of the earth to hundreds of thousands of years, they stretched it beyond human comprehension, which was highly disconcerting to many people.

Silliman was aware of the conundrum that fossils presented in relation to the age of the earth. What was troubling was not so much their antiquity or that they were found in varying layers of rock but that many of them differed greatly from existing animals. That meant either that their identical descendants were alive on some unexplored part of the globe—in this category was Jefferson's *Incognitum* browsing on the Great Plains—or that they had gone extinct. Extinction posed a major challenge to theologians because it meant that God had made creatures that had been allowed to die out, raising the possibility that Noah had left some species behind when he closed the door on the ark.

Then, too, there was the idea of the "watchmaker God" as set forth by William Paley (1743–1805), a bishop in England. His book, *Natural Theology, or Evidences of the Existence and Attributes of the Deity*, was published in 1802 and was very influential on both sides of the Atlantic. The Percival family owned a copy.[13] In *Natural Theology*, Paley argued by analogy that the movement of heavenly bodies was so regular it was like a finely designed watch that, once built and wound, would go on without the continuing intervention of the watchmaker. Again it was the existence of fossils that undercut Paley's ideas because if the watchmaker made the world perfect, why did species go extinct? Heavenly bodies conformed much better to Paley's ideas than earthly bodies, which were anything but perfect.

It was at the venerable University of Edinburgh that Silliman heard of startling speculations about the creation of the earth as formulated by the Scotsman James Hutton (1726–1797) and the German Abraham Gottlob Werner (1749–1817). Hutton's idea that the earth's core was molten and heat was the energy behind the creation of the earth would eventually win the day over Werner's idea of the surface of the earth being precipitated out of a vast primordial sea. However, this was not a winner-take-all contest between two feuding scientists. Both had much to offer, and both were mistaken in many ways. Yet right or wrong, they helped spur the growth of geology as a science, although the controversy (carried on by their followers) would not come to an end for decades.

Hutton was a geologist, physician, naturalist, and member of the Scottish enlightenment who conceived of the earth as a dynamic, self-regulating system. Although some of his ideas were not original, the way he put them together led to a unique conception of how the earth was formed. There were underlying fixed laws that directed change, but the process was slow, repetitive, and ongoing—the same in the present as in the past. Therefore, the earth had to be very old. Hutton's idea of uniform change conflicted with the Biblical idea of everything being made in six days followed by a catastrophic flood. In fact, in Hutton's words, the earth had "no vestige of a beginning—no prospect of an end."[14]

Hutton had become interested in geology when he set out to improve the agricultural production of his two farms in Scotland, one in the lowlands and the other in the highlands. In the process, he took a radically different look at the soil and rocks, writing in a letter that he had "become very fond of studying the surface of the earth, and was looking with anxious curiosity into every pit or ditch or bed of a river that fell in his way."[15] This led to years of rigorous fieldwork all over the British Isles that revealed to him that the same forces were at work everywhere. These uniform forces included erosion, sedimentation, uplift, and volcanism. In a drawing of what came to be called an unconformity that Hutton discovered in Jedburgh in 1787, the two top horizontal layers rest on a vertical layer of a different type of sandstone called greywacke.[16] To Hutton, this abrupt reorientation of layers proved that there was no single catastrophic flood, writing, "I rejoiced at my good fortune in stumbling upon an object so interesting in the natural history of the earth."

Although Hutton did not overtly challenge religious leaders, writing that his work "in no way related to the morality of human actions," his ideas were viewed as deistic, even verging on atheistic.[17] It was not just that he considered the earth to be very old but that it was endless. The first idea struck at the heart of the Book of Genesis. The second struck at the heart of the Book of Revelation (6:12), in which the sixth seal prophesies that at the apocalypse there will be a severe earthquake, the sky will recede like a rolled-up scroll, and every mountain and island will be removed from its place. To Hutton, geological processes were of the same kind and intensity over time, the earth was dynamic and rocks changed cyclically—from magma cooling into igneous rock, eroding into sedimentary rock, melting back into magma—over and over again. Hutton's ideas were aligned with what was called Plutonism, named after Pluto, the underworld god, or alternatively, Vulcanism, after Vulcan, the god of the forge and metalworking.

These gods of heat stood in opposition to Neptune, the god of water. The school of geological speculation known as Neptunism was put forward by Werner, who was head of mining at the prestigious mining academy at Freiberg in Saxony. However, the main focus of Werner's research was not Neptunism, which pre-dated him. Instead, it was the nature of rock formations as well as how to identify minerals by external characteristics, such as color, taste, texture, smell, and hardness. Because Werner was a brilliant scientist who had the practicality of a miner, the men who studied under him were the most highly trained mineralo-gists in the world, Alexander von Humboldt among them.[18] It was Werner's mineral-identification system that Silliman brought back with him to Yale and taught to generations of students, one of them being Percival, who learned it thoroughly. According to Mott T. Greene in his book *Geology in the Nineteenth Century*, "Werner's was a quaint system, cumbersome and discursive, requiring a great deal of effort to learn, especially the retraining of the senses to distinguish the varieties of character and color. But combined with similar discrimination of other characters, it was, in his time, the most powerful tool yet devised for the identification of minerals in the field."[19]

Werner thought, erroneously, that all minerals had precipitated out of a vast primordial sea that covered the earth. Supposedly the water in that sea was denser than present-day seawater, which is why minerals and rocks could precipitate out so easily. The earth's core was formed by sedimentation and was exposed when the wa-ters receded, thereby revealing continents. Subsequently, the earth was covered by a worldwide flood that added new layers of rock. There were many gaping holes in this idea. One was the question, Where did the floodwaters recede to? Some of Werner's followers, including Silliman, speculated there might be vast underground chasms into which the water drained, an idea with precedent in the Book of Revelation (12:16), where the earth opens its mouth and swallows up a mighty river. Another challenge was the role of volcanoes. Because Werner and his followers did not believe that the earth had a molten core, volcanoes had to be caused by fires smoldering in underground coal beds. It followed that lava was sedimentary rock that had melted in these fires and then been ejected.[20]

At the University of Edinburgh, the battle between Neptunism and Plutonism was waged by two professors acting in the roles of defense attorneys: John Murray made the case for Werner and Neptunism, and John Playfair made the case for Hutton and Plutonism. Their disputations were carried on in books and lectures.[21] For the students in Edinburgh, Silliman among them, it was an exhilarating and confusing time because there were many logical flaws. Proof was hard to find, if it could be found at all—the evidence being buried deep. When Silliman returned to Yale, he was on Werner's side, not Hutton's. Faced with incomplete and conflicting evidence that was easy to misinterpret, it seemed to Silliman that a world shaped by water was more plausible than a world shaped by fire. According to Herbert Hovenkamp in his book *Science and Religion in America, 1800–1860*, even after the publication of Playfair's book that clarified Hutton's thinking, "most geologists chose to reject Hutton's ideas as too radical and used instead the rather simple Wernerian classification system and the concomitant theories about geologic formation."[22]

In Edinburgh, Silliman had been impressed with the Salisbury Crags that towered over the city in exactly the same way that East Rock and West Rock towered over New Haven. In fact, they looked so similar with their columnar form that Silliman was "ready to say that they were broken from the same mass." After his return to Yale, he set about exploring the traprock, referring to it by the Scottish term *whin stone* or the Swedish term *trap* (both meaning step or stair), which he determined was igneous. In his "Sketch of the Mineralogy of the Town of New Haven," presented in 1806, he wrote that the rocks had "actually been melted in the bowels of the earth and ejected among the superior strata by the force of subterraneous fire, but never erupted like lava, cooling under the pressure of the superincumbent strata and therefore compact or nonvesicular, its present form being due to erosion."[23] He did not explain what he meant by subterraneous fire, although he did not mean to imply that the earth had a molten core. He also stated that European scientists were divided between Neptunism and Plutonism. Attempting to stay on the high ground of fact, he wrote, "Perhaps it would be more correct to apologize for having digressed at all into theories of the earth where we usually find so much that is visionary, hypothetical or false, than to persist farther in speculations which must at last end where they began, in doubt and uncertainty." Yet his choice of words in the essay revealed his dedication to Werner, for example, his description of the rocks in New Haven, which were as old as Creation, being worn down by the same play of elemental forces that were wearing down the Alps and the Andes. In no way was this Hutton's view of an earth that continually repaired itself.[24] According to Chandos Brown, Silliman had returned from Europe essentially unchanged: "Though his horizon had broadened, he had not succumbed to the pernicious doctrines that lurked so dangerously near to the surface of contemporary science." Yet Silliman was not an ideologue. As his teaching career progressed, he mixed and matched from competing geological ideas, providing space in *The American Journal of Science and Arts* for the opposition. Brown concludes, "Chemistry and mineralogy would soon stand in need of a theoretical framework, and they would have one. For the present, however, Silliman was convinced that there was no overwhelming reason to examine the history of the earth in any light other than that afforded by Christian revelation."[25]

From then on Silliman's career was *literally* meteoric. At about six thirty on the morning of December 14, 1807, when it was still dark, a huge fireball streaked across the sky of New England, traveling from northeast to southwest. One witness likened it to that "of the sun seen through the mist."[26] Three loud booms shook the land as the meteoroid exploded with a force that could be heard many miles away, scattering fragments over a wide swath of Weston, Connecticut. When Silliman heard about the event a few days later, he immediately set out with the Yale professor James Kingsley to interview eyewitnesses and collect samples. They found scavengers hard at work picking up fragments in the hope of finding precious metals, subjecting them, as Silliman put it, "to all the tortures of ancient alchemy," which included crucibles, forges, and anvils. Instead, he and Kingsley took a scientific approach and conducted a chemical analysis, determining the pieces to be a nonmetallic aggregation of dust particles. Their analysis was published by the American Philosophical Society in March 1808 and then reprinted in Europe, where there was much scientific interest in meteorites. Just five years before, in 1803, a similar fireball had exploded into thousands of pieces in Normandy, France. Up until then scientists had been dubious that rocks could fall from space, contending that their origin had to be terrestrial, perhaps coming from a very distant volcano belching out boulders. Because the fireball had hit in early afternoon, there were many reliable witnesses, prompting the French Academy of Sciences to send a young scientist, Jean-Baptiste Biot, to investigate. It is likely that Silliman had read Biot's report because Silliman wrote: "In Europe I had become acquainted with meteorites and the phenomena that usually attend their fall. I did not dream of being favored by an event of this kind in my own vicinity and occurring on a scale truly magnificent."[27]

The Weston fireball helped to make Silliman famous in Connecticut and increased the interest of the citizenry in the connection between astronomy, chemistry, and mineralogy. Silliman's only regret was that the largest fragment, which was 35.5 pounds, was sold by a farmer to George Gibbs, a wealthy mineralogist who had traveled in Asia and Europe amassing a rock collection that was world class. However, in 1810, the year that Percival was a freshman, Gibbs offered to place his rock collection at Yale, an offer that was readily accepted and that led to its being purchased by the college in 1825. So Silliman got his fragment, and Percival and hundreds of other students gained access to a mineral cabinet of approximately twenty thousand specimens. This was extremely important to the advancement of geology at Yale because such a collection enabled a student to see, smell, touch, and even taste minerals and rocks, which was essential in learning how to identify them in the field. To teach geology without a cabinet of minerals was analogous to teaching anatomy without a body.

Curiously, when Percival was an adult he wrote a poem titled "The Vision" about an event in his childhood that may have been the Weston fireball. Over the years it had recurred in his dreams like an evil portent that troubled his sleep. The star he saw had a "train directed at the earth." It spread out and grew crimson "till a whole quarter of the heavens was red and glowing like a furnace" while he heard a sound "like far-off winds or smothered flames roaring in caves." Given his imagination and the fact that he most likely had read about the fireball, it is possible he did not actually witness it. Percival himself seemed uncertain about whether the memory was real or fanciful.[28] The fireball was not the only astronomical event that eventually found expression in either Percival's poetry or scientific papers. So too did the aurora borealis in the night sky as well as oblique beams of light that he saw shooting from a bank of storm clouds just as the sun was setting—an observation on the nature of reflection that found its way into Silliman's *American Journal of Science and Arts*.[29]

It was not Silliman's investigations of fireballs or discoveries in geology that would elevate him into the pantheon of American science. Above all else, teaching was at the heart of his life, and he did it very well, training generations of future scientists. In 1809, Samuel Griswold Goodrich, a friend of Percival, attended one of Silliman's chemistry lectures at Yale and was much impressed by the experiments that were done: "The lights were put out. A piece of wire was coiled in a glass jar filled with oxygen. A light was applied—and fizz—fizz, went the wire, actually burning like a witch-quill!" More experiments followed, convincing everyone in attendance "that the new science was not to be feared, as smelling of necromancy," but that in fact it was honest science. "What wonders were thus disclosed to the astonished people! By means of blowpipes, flasks and crucibles, all nature seemed to be transformed as if by the spells of a sorcerer. The four old-fashioned elements were changed—proved, in short to be imposters, having been passed off from time immemorial as solid, substantial honest elements, while they were in fact, each and all, only a parcel of compounds!"[30]

In 1810, when Percival entered Yale and met Benjamin Silliman, he had no idea what profession to pursue. While the majority of the students were headed for the ministry, Percival was too much of a skeptic and freethinker for that. There was no career path for geology or chemistry other than to teach it. Geology would not become a recognized profession until the finding of ore became critically important to the industrial revolution. If a salary paid by a mining company or the government indicated an amateur geologist was now a professional, then Percival would have been among the first, along with a handful of men who conducted the state mineral and geological surveys beginning in the 1830s.

Every morning before class, Percival would take a long solitary walk, returning to the lecture room prior to the professor's arrival to jot down his thoughts and review his notes. William Chauncey Fowler, a classmate, wrote, "On one occasion, he read to me before the College recitation at eleven o'clock, seventeen stanzas of nine lines each, composed that very morning." To Fowler, it was as if Percival was communing with the divine, "his face shone as if he had just come down from the sacred mount, flushed by an interview with the mythological immortals. The readiness and continuity of his poetic associations were marvelous." When the lecture commenced, Percival would listen with a level of concentration that astounded the other students and intimidated some of the lecturers. When the lecture was finished, he would head out again, sometimes up West Rock, sometimes up East Rock, sometimes along the shore, always alone. He wrote in a poem titled "Love of Study" the following prose opening: "There are many youths, and some men, who most earnestly devote themselves to solitary studies, from the mere love of the pursuit."[31]

Several of his student notebooks are at the Beinecke Archives at Yale, written in what Ward described as Percival's "cramped, close chirography." One contains his meticulous notes on eighty-four chemistry lectures given by Silliman. Another is a three-hundred-page notebook that provides insights into what Percival was learning and reading:

> It contains very careful notes of "*Mr. Silliman's Private Lectures on Mineralogy*," of "*Mr. Kingsley's Lectures on History*," of a "*Treatise on Husbandry*," a full treatise on Botany with extensive notes of Dr. Ives' Lectures; "*A View of the Natural Orders of Linnæus from the Encyclopædia Britannica*"; "*Additional Genera from Shaw's General Zöology*"; the "*Natural Families of Vegetables*"; a Continuation of Professor Silliman's Lectures on Chemistry; and very complete notes of "*A System of Chemistry by John Murray, Vol. II.*" There is another

book devoted entirely to *"An Epitome of Wilson's Ornithology"*; and another partially filled with a work on *"Zoology compiled from Shaw, Buffin, and Pennant."* These extensive studies of an undergraduate confirm the remark of one of his classmates: "I never knew one who could acquire correct knowledge quicker than Percival." [32]

To that above list it should be noted that after his graduation, Percival added three books by John Playfair, the defender of Hutton, to his rapidly growing library. As much as he respected Silliman, Percival was beginning to understand that while water played a major role in sedimentation and erosion, it was not the engine that powered the ongoing creation of the earth. That engine was heat deep underground. [33]

This chapter began with a description of Silliman's portrait. There are two additional aspects to the portrait that are unseen. The painter facing Silliman on the opposite side of the easel was Samuel F. B. Morse, who would also have a major effect on science, indeed on the world. Not long before painting Silliman, Morse had completed Percival's portrait, capturing the physical essence of the Byronesque romantic poet—the intense stare, the slightly furrowed forehead with a receding hairline, the high cravat rising up to his jaw. Whereas Silliman looked self-assured, Percival looked haunted. About the portrait, Percival wrote to a friend, "I have lately had some intimacy with Morse, while taking a portrait of my phiz [face]. Your judgment is not far from correct. He is a good artist, and has a mind much above the common level." [34] Morse had graduated from Yale in 1810 (the year Percival began) and then went to Europe to study art. While at Yale, he had attended Silliman's lectures, which made an indelible impression on him. He had also gone on geology trips with Silliman. Seven years after finishing the portrait of Silliman, Morse would begin work on inventing the telegraph and the dot-and-dash code that would bear his name.

The second aspect in the painting is West Rock itself. In an editorial for the *American Journal of Science and Arts*, Silliman wrote, "If the painter were always a geologist, his sketches of rock scenery, and of ever varying outline of a landscape, as it is seen in hills, plains, valleys, waters and mountains would assume a verisimilitude, depending on physical laws. . . . Were the geologist a painter, he would breathe into his faithful graphic outlines, the living spirit of the sublime and the beautiful; as well as his understanding [of geology]; and were the power of poetry added . . . the subject would then assume its highest interest, and attract attention from a large class of admirers." Redolent of the potent combination of romanticism and science, Silliman's statement moved West Rock from the background to the foreground, making of geology the door to the far below and the great beyond.[35]

THREE

Physician, Heal Thyself

As graduation approached, Percival was disappointed to learn he had not been selected to deliver the valedictory address even though he was at the top of his class. The reason was his inability to speak loudly due to the damage to his vocal cords caused by meningitis. Describing Percival's voice as "sibilant," a fellow student recalled that during Percival's senior year President Dwight had reprimanded him in class, saying, "Read up louder, Percival. You have nothing to be ashamed of." When Dwight assigned him a graduation speech of lesser importance, Percival was determined to do his best, confiding in a friend, "I took much pains to prepare myself; I practiced myself in distinctness; I articulated my words." The upshot was he delivered the speech so well that Dwight regretted having chosen someone else for the highest honor.[1]

The subject Percival was assigned was to compare the value of a scientific versus a military reputation. This was a typical subject assigned to a promising senior, suitable for showing off his abilities in reasoning and rhetoric to an appreciative audience. However, Percival's approach was not typical. He began in a straightforward way, using Isaac Newton as the supreme example of the man of science whose "astonishing labours" and "the strong light in which his discoveries were beheld" brought him deserved fame. "Not only are the labours of the man of science more valuable, but his reputation is more lasting," Percival emphasized. "The warrior may be for a time more celebrated, his name may be recalled from one country to another; title, honour may be given him; eulogies may be pronounced; everything for a time may wear the appearance of splendid gratitude, but the storm of his reputation will soon be over." Only the fame of the man of science would remain.[2]

Then Percival shifted to a related subject—the nature of genius —which he described from his own experience as a "kind of felicitous spirit or energy" enabling its possessor to gather and analyze facts in a way that led to the perception of overarching systems. This is what Newton had accomplished in his *Philosophiæ Naturalis Principia Mathematica*. To Percival, genius was "the peculiar contribution of the mind by which it is justified by a strength and energy that enables it to persevere and penetrate, and of an acuteness of perception by which it readily describes the analogies and differences between the various objects presented to its senses." Genius led to "discovering general conclusions from particular facts and melding scattered elements into systems." This was why the fame of the man of science was superior to the fame of the warrior.[3]

These ideas were seminal for Percival, shaping his scientific career. Twenty years later, in 1835, when Percival began his work on the geological survey of Connecticut, uppermost in his mind would be the search for an overarching system to explain the nature of rock formations based on the "particular facts" he had gathered in his research. In a letter to a Connecticut legislator, Percival wrote that his goal was to "determine the actual system of arrangement—a system that once determined will last as long as time, or at least as long as the human race."[4]

Percival would also remain focused on the idea of genius, expressing in numerous poems his frustration that it—by which he meant himself—was not appreciated. As much as he prized genius, he was pained by the loneliness it inflicted on him. Yet he was proud that genius lifted him far above lesser men who only wanted to be entertained, not enlightened. In the poem "Genius Waking," he wrote in the first stanza:

Thine was once the highest pinion
　In the midway air;
With a proud and sure dominion,
　Thou didst upward bear;

Like the herald, winged with lightning,
   From the Olympian throne,
Ever mounting, ever brightening,
   Thou wert there alone.[5]

Unfortunately, the period between Percival's graduation and the beginning of his geological fieldwork would not be a time of systems but a lack thereof. The power of genius would still be there, "winged with lightning," but it was often out of control. The chaos started immediately upon graduation with his extreme mood swings—from sublime highs that made every detail of the world incandescent to suicidal lows in which death in multiple guises became his best friend.

Percival had hoped to be appointed a tutor at Yale, a position that was a combination of mentoring and lecturing. Tutors usually went on to become professors, as had been the case with Benjamin Silliman. Partially because of Percival's difficulty with public speaking, President Dwight did not offer him the position, leaving him dangerously adrift. From then on, he would start projects and abruptly abandon them; he would take jobs and immediately quit; he would fall in love and be spurned. Horace Hooker, a childhood friend from Kensington who had graduated with Percival from Yale, recalled that Percival came to his room in New Haven nearly every day during this period. "He used to come in the morning with a plan for a new book, or a new poem, or with new theories concerning the studies in which he was engaged. He would enlarge upon them brilliantly, exhaustively, seeming to have the subject entirely at hand, and when he went away, left the impression that he was set about the immediate execution of his plan; but when he came again the next day he had a new project, and the one discussed so earnestly and feasibly the day before had been abandoned."[6]

Having been denied the position of tutor, Percival cast about for a profession, taking to heart the blunt advice Dwight had given him his senior year: "Percival, you must engage in some active employment, or you are a ruined man."[7] He even considered the ministry, but although he believed in God as a transcendent power, he was repulsed by some of the earthly aspects of Christianity that tended toward superstition. Having as high a regard for Olympus as Jerusalem, he decided that the cool rationality of law might be a better choice. Off and on for two years, he studied law in Philadelphia, during which time he supplemented his income by tutoring the children of a judge and later of a lawyer, but the pay was poor, about which he often complained. Furthermore, he found law to be boring. He passed the bar but never practiced.

Instead, Percival turned to medicine, setting his mind to follow in his father's footsteps. He began by studying the texts in the medical library of Dr. Josiah Ward, the well-respected physician who had taken over the medical practice of Percival's father in Kensington and Berlin. Percival went through his library with such speed and thoroughness that Ward suggested it might be wise for him to return to New Haven to study under Dr. Eli Ives, who had helped establish the medical school and was an expert in botany and the use of medicinal plants. For some unknown reason, Percival did not immediately take Ward's advice, choosing to go back to Philadelphia, where in addition to studying law, he attended medical lectures at the University of Pennsylvania. However, in the spring of 1816 Percival was ready to return and commence studying with Ives, explaining to him in a letter why he had not done so earlier: "I knew that medicine was the profession most congenial to my mind. I believed it the most useful, and I think I should have eagerly pursued it, had my health been good, and had I seen my way open; but ill health, low spirits, and embarrassments will dishearten."[8]

As an undergraduate, Percival had studied botany under Dr. Ives. He had also been Ives's patient when he came down with measles. For him to be under Ives's compassionate purview at this chaotic point of his life should have been a very good turn of events. Ives was a highly respected teacher and practitioner. Tall, thin, and unassuming, Ives's physical appearance belied the fact that he was known to his colleagues as a very hard worker who would tend to patients at all hours of the day or night. His teaching style was more relaxed than Silliman's, with his blue cloak casually askew as he told stories from his experience as a physician, often with a

FIG. 3.1. Nathaniel Jocelyn, *Portrait of Eli Ives*, 1827. Oil on canvas. Yale Medical School, Yale University Art Gallery. Eli Ives was a physician who helped established the medical school at Yale. He mentored Percival in medicine and hired him to create a botanical garden for the benefit of Yale students, but unfortunately the project came to nothing.

dollop of humor. One such story was on the therapeutic use of cobwebs: "Cobweb is given in intermittent doses of five grains, which is as powerful as twenty grains; or give the spider itself, or which perhaps is as good, make the patient think he is about to take the spider."[9]

Because Percival was strapped for money, he suggested to Dr. Ives that in return for being mentored in medicine he work as his assistant on various botanical projects. Ives had a large private garden near his home and office on the corner of Wall and Temple Streets. The garden was filled with herbs and medicinal plants, extensive grape arbors, fruit trees, vegetables, and potatoes. As a friend expressed it, Ives "prescribed with a hoe from the resources of his wonderful botanical garden."[10] However, Ives had a far greater dream. He wanted to plant a botanical garden to be used for medical education and research at Yale. Botanical gardens, also called physic gardens, had long been connected to monasteries and universities in Europe to educate students in the healing properties of plants. Students at the University of Pennsylvania had access to John Bartram's botanical garden, the largest in the nation. A friend of Benjamin Franklin, Bartram had collected and catalogued plants throughout the colonies, adding to them plants procured from Europe and Asia. In contrast, students at Yale's struggling medical school had nothing but Ives's backyard plot. The problem Ives faced was that establishing a significant botanical garden took much time and was costly because plants had to be purchased from around the world and greenhouses had to be built. Nevertheless, Ives had resolutely begun planning and had already received over a thousand varieties from the king of France, which is why he readily agreed to Percival's proposal to work as his assistant. For his part, Percival was delighted because "it gave full scope to his love of botany."[11]

One plant in which Ives was particularly interested was foxglove. With its tall spikes in many shades of pink, red, and white, foxglove was grown both for the beauty of its bell-shaped flowers and for digitalis, used for heart conditions. Although, at that time, physicians knew it could be deadly and that all parts of the plant were toxic, they did not know what was the correct dosage or when it should be administered, the result being that its effect on a patient was wildly unpredictable. Concerned about possible impurity as well as the lack of standardization, Dr. Ives wrote that digitalis "is probably the most dangerous narcotic we possess."[12]

Percival also helped in the research Ives was conducting on the medicinal properties of tea, wine, and coffee. They concluded that tea was good for inflammatory diseases but could make nervous disorders worse. Wine in moderation was good; furthermore, it was Biblically approved. As for coffee, it had long been known to be a strong stimulant. Percival was solely responsible for the research on coffee, which would prove to be valuable, even lifesaving, to him later on.[13]

Because Ives had an extensive botanical library, he also asked Percival to translate from Latin *A Systematic Arrangement and Description of the Plants of North America* by Frederick Pursh, which had recently been published in London.[14] Percival's skills as a translator may have spurred him to write some poems on botanical themes, including "On Finding the Anemone Hepatica; The Earliest Flower of Spring," "A Tulip Blossomed," and "To the Houstonia Cerulea," commonly known as the bluet, which carpeted New England each spring. In that poem, he included a footnote that "the botanical allusions perhaps will not be fully relished by those who have not examined the structure of the flower." Among the allusions were the "downy stigma," the "atom seeds of fertilizing dust," and the "lurking anthers."[15]

With Ives's encouragement things were going very well for Percival. But once again, a contagious disease upended Percival's life. He fell seriously ill with typhoid fever, becoming Ives's patient instead of his assistant. When he finally recovered, "he could not be induced to resume his duties." The research on the effects of tea, wine, and coffee, the Latin translation, and the planting all came to a halt.[16] The varieties from France ended up in Ives's own backyard garden.

Percival's intermittent medical studies did not prevent him from eventually receiving his medical degree in 1820 from Yale, where he subsequently lectured in anatomy. Dr. Ives was deeply impressed with Percival's abilities regardless of his deficits. In a glowing letter of recommendation, dated September 21, 1821, Ives wrote: "This certifies that Dr. James Gates Percival has passed through the academic and medical institutions in this college with much credit to himself and satisfaction to his instructors. He is a universal scholar, and as a naturalist is scarcely excelled by any person of his age in the United States. As a medical scholar I may safely say that, from the commencement of the Medical Institution in this place, no one in the examination for a degree of Doctor of Medicine has appeared better than Dr. J. G. Percival."[17]

Percival's first published poems appeared in the short-lived magazine *The Microscope*, printed in New Haven by a few of his acquaintances, who dubbed themselves "a Fraternity of Gentlemen," although the unnamed editor was actually Cornelius Tuthill. The name of the publication was related to the magazine's goal "of examining objects nearer than can be done with the distinctness of vision by the naked eye." *The Microscope* did not print the names of its contributors, instead using either initials or aliases, such as Horatio and Morpheus. Without attribution, Percival's lengthy poem "The Suicide" took up two entire issues in May and June. Not until the last issue, in September 1820, did Tuthill acknowledge Percival's major contribution to the publication.[18]

By then, Percival had decided to print a small book of poetry at his own expense. Titled simply *Poems*, it appeared in July 1821 and included the first part of the poem "Prometheus." It also included "The Suicide," from which Percival felt the need to distance himself a little, reassuring his readers that it was not wholly autobiographical. In fact, suicide was not uncommon in this period, one of the most disturbing being that of Silliman's young relative, James Noyes. To everyone's dismay, during a religious revival at Yale in 1815, Percival's senior year, Noyes drowned himself after having reached the tragically misguided conclusion that he was not worthy of salvation. Percival had been criticized for not including an overt Christian message about the nature of sin and salvation in the poem, perchance increasing the hopelessness of his readers, which is why he wrote in the preface, "Perhaps some apology may be demanded for *The Suicide*. I can only say that it is intended as a picture of the horror and wretchedness of a youth ruined by early perversion, and of the causes of that perversion. It is not without a moral to those who see it." In one stanza, he pondered his multiple failures:

Ah! Who can bear the self-abhorring thought
Of time, chance, talent, wasted—who can think
Of friendship, love, fame, science, gone to naught,
And not in hopeless desperation sink.[19]

In "The Suicide," he also wrote of his bitterness about being jilted in love. While numerous stories about Percival made the point that he had great difficulty dealing with women, often falling silent in their presence, apparently that difficulty did not prevent him from falling in love. There was his romance with a young woman in Berlin named Mary, the sister of Samuel Griswold Goodrich, who became engaged to another man. There was also his romance with one of the young women he tutored in Philadelphia. He proposed to her by letter, to which he received a polite refusal from a third party who wrote that the woman considered him only a friend. His infatuation spurred him to write love poetry filled with standard romantic tropes, such as raven hair, dark lashes that fluttered, and "bosoms lit with ethereal flame" (see plate 10). It also led him to write furious poems about rejection. For example, the poem "She's Gone" begins with the line, "She's gone, the idol of my heart, She's gone at last forever," and ends with, "Then go, thou false unmeaning thing, / Go, and begone forever! / Shalt thou again my bosom wring, / And steal my tears?—no never."

Some people expressed doubt as to whether Percival actually attempted suicide, but the Reverend Royal Robbins recalled that once when he and Percival were walking together in Kensington, Percival suddenly broke into a run and dashed his head against a stone wall. There were also many rumors that circulated among his friends and family about his plans to overdose on opium, stab or shoot himself, or drown himself in the rising tide of the Bay of Fundy. The poem "The Suicide" seems to verify that all those forms of suicide did cross his tortured mind, for he wrote of the "death-winged ball" that could pierce his brain, and the knife "that can loose the shackles of my soul," the opiate "that can ease my every pain," and the "smiling surface of the wave" that invited him to endless sleep. Perhaps the most reliable evidence is Percival's confession to Charles Shepard, the Yale professor who worked with him on the Connecticut geological survey in 1835, that there were times when on their field trips he would see a dark mine shaft or blast furnace and the thought would spring up that he should throw himself in.

Of all the stories (bordering on the apocryphal) about Percival's suicide attempts, the one about an overdose of opium is most likely true for two reasons: the details came from Percival's brother Oswin; and the antidote—very strong coffee in copious amounts to counteract the depressant effect of opium—could only have been suggested by Percival himself, stemming from his research with Dr. Ives. Opium was legal, readily available, and often prescribed by physicians. Dr. Ives recommended its use for many diseases and had even presented a paper to a medical society on a failed attempt to cure a seven-year-old boy of hydrophobia by means of opium and mercury.[20] At the time of Percival's overdose, he was so depressed that his family and friends were extremely concerned. When he disappeared, apparently to go to the nearby town of Farmington to buy opium, they began to search for him:

> Suddenly he appeared in the orchard near the house, and was seen walking to and fro, holding his hand to his mouth, as if he were chewing something. A little later, his brother, returning from the mill, saw persons leading him about the yard. He had taken an overdose, and was in a pale sweat and great pain. His brother asked him if he had been chewing opium. He replied that he had; and to his brother's further question whether he had any more, he drew a small ball from his vest pocket and threw it violently upon the ground. He was taken to the house, and the servant was ordered to prepare some very strong coffee as an antidote to the poison; and he soon grew better. But the spirit of the madman was yet upon him; and his next plan was to go to the Bay of Fundy and let the swiftly rising tide engulf him.[21]

Although Percival's suicidal thinking did not end with strong coffee, fortunately it *did* end, abruptly and permanently. Planning another attempt, this time with pistols, Percival suddenly realized the pressure in his head was gone and his obsession with death had vanished. As he later told a friend, he said to himself, "I will live and take what God gives me." Although he remained melancholic, he never attempted suicide again.

In the early 1820s, Percival made an effort to establish himself as a physician in Kensington, using the old homestead for his office. Tragically, an epidemic broke out in town "which baffled the skill of the best physicians." One family with seven children fell ill, and Dr. Josiah Ward, who was treating approximately sixty cases and was overwhelmed, sought Percival's assistance. The family lived near the millpond close to Percival's home and the general opinion was the children had fallen ill due to wading in the mud. According to Catharine North in her book *The History of Berlin Connecticut*, New England spotted fever or typhus was prevalent in the area in the 1820s, so much so it was called the Berlin fever. Many people attributed it to stagnant water; one citizen of Berlin expressed the opinion that the swamp was the source of the illness and should be drained. This was at the same time as the outbreak of typhus syncopalis—meningitis—in nearby Middletown described in detail by Dr. Thomas Miner.[22]

There is an eerie similarity between the deaths of Dr. Ward in 1825 and James Gates Percival's father in 1807. In December 1806, Dr. Percival had ridden by horseback to attend critically ill patients; at one point he fell asleep by the fireplace in a patient's home. Given the circumstances, his exhaustion was to be expected, but its sudden onset was unusual. So also, Dr. Ward rode day and night to visit his patients "until he was so exhausted that he would sleep anywhere, even on horseback." While tending to a minister and his family, Dr. Ward fell asleep on the church steps. "He awoke with a chill—the precursor of the fever, from which in his worn condition he would never rally." Dr. Ward died in August 1825 at the age of forty-three.[23] Just as Dr. Percival had awoken with a chill, returned home, and spread the disease to his family, so also did Dr. Ward. Two of his children died and his wife was critically ill.

So severe was the epidemic in Berlin that according to one witness the main street "was strewed with tan bark in order to deaden the sound of the wagon wheels, and the hearse was not put in its place at all so steady was its use."[24] This gives credence to the epidemic being meningitis because people suffering from the disease are often intolerant of loud noises and light.

As to the family that Dr. Ward had asked Percival to treat, five of the boys, from two to twelve years of age, died in quick succession.[25] He was also caring for other patients with the disease, five of whom died on one day. According to Julius Ward in his biography of Percival, "Such mortality alarmed him. He was unable to bear the responsibility laid upon the physician. He said afterwards to Dr. Barnes, 'I could not bear to have people looking to me for relief and not be able to relieve them.'" That Percival was reluctant to provide medical help is borne out in a letter he wrote to his friend Dr. George Hayward: "The physician in this place died about two weeks since; and I have been compelled, against my wishes and in spite of my refusal, to attend to some patients."[26] In light of the serious diseases he himself had suffered (meningitis, measles, and typhoid), which no physician could cure or relieve, it is possible that Percival was looking inward. As a scholar of *Prometheus Bound* by Aeschylus, which he translated in its entirety, Percival may have had in mind the lines, "Like an unskilled physician, fallen ill, you lose heart and cannot discover by what remedies to cure your own disease." The idea of the sick physician also appears in the Bible as "physician, heal thyself."[27]

There is little indication in his poetry about the emotional upheaval in his life caused by the death of the five children who lived near the millpond except for one exquisite poem titled "The Death of a Child," in which Percival poignantly wrote about the passing of a small boy he perceived as his son (excerpt):

I sat beside the pillow of a child,—
His dying pillow,—and I watched the ebb
Of his last fluttering breath. All tranquilly

He passed away, and not a murmur came
From his white lips. A film crept o'er his eye,
But did not all conceal it, and at times
The darkness stole away, and he looked out
Serenely, with an innocent smile, as if
Pleased with an infant's toy; and there was then
A very delicate flush upon his cheek
Like the new edging of a damask-rose,
When first the bud uncloses. As I watched,
I caught at these awakenings with better hope,
And yielding to the longing of my heart,
Fancied I saw him opening from a trance,
And with a gentle effort shaking off
The oppression of a dream. A moment more,
And the film mantled o'er his eye again,
And the faint redness left his faltering lips,
And backward to its centre in the heart
The crimson current rallied, leaving him
Like a chill statue, cold and pale.[28]

Although Julius Ward indicated in his biography of Percival that the tragedy in Kensington led to his giving up medicine, that was not entirely the case. Before that, he had tried to establish a medical practice in Charleston, South Carolina, beginning in December 1821. He had gone to Charleston in an effort to start anew in a warmer, hopefully more congenial climate.[29] For a brief time, he was happy, writing some of the best poetry of his life and attempting to earn money by giving botanical lectures, but he could not make a living as a physician. As he told a friend, "When a person is really ill he will not send for a poet to cure him." Percival returned to New Haven and attempted to set up a practice there, but not long after, he wrote to Samuel Gilman, a friend in Charleston, "I cannot boast of one single call, not even to tie up a cut finger."[30]

Again acquaintances came to his aid. John C. Calhoun, who had graduated from Yale and was Secretary of War, arranged for Percival to be appointed as both a surgeon and a professor of chemistry at West Point. He arrived in May 1824 and hated it immediately, finding the situation untenable and declaring vociferously that he was no chemist. He was transferred in July to Boston as an assistant surgeon in charge of examination of recruits. He hated that as well and resigned less than a month later. Subsequently, he asked to be reinstated, but his military medical career was over.[31]

While Percival never practiced after the epidemic in Kensington, neither did he drop the "Dr." from his name, remaining loyal to the profession. In 1829, having returned briefly to Kensington, he wrote out a will, leaving his estate to his mother, but in the event she predeceased him, it was to go to the Medical Society of Connecticut to fund a prize for the best dissertation on the physical and physico-moral education of children. The will stated that "enlightened physicians" were the best judges of health and morals, "and that no other inquiry can be of more vital importance." The two executors were Dr. Eli Ives and Dr. George Hayward, a highly respected surgeon who had met Percival during the brief period when he lived in Boston and who had interceded on Percival's behalf with editors and publishers. To Hayward, Percival was a wonder, writing that his "literary and scientific attainments were greater than those of any man I ever knew."[32]

FOUR

Poetry as a Way of Being

In the letter Percival wrote to Samuel Gilman about his abysmal efforts to establish a medical practice, first in Charleston and then in New Haven, he admitted with regret that he was not fitted for such work. Yet he was not discouraged because he had "two strings to my bow, perhaps twenty, and if one won't shoot, perhaps another will." The string he resolved to shoot with was poetry. "I sincerely believe I must be contented to live as peaceable as I can with myself and the world, and put my ambition in writing as much and as well as I can. I find a positive pleasure in writing. I seem to have heart when I have poured myself out on paper. There is something which proves to me Descartes' proposition, 'Cogito ergo sum.' I shall write, then, as long as I can or until I begin to damn myself by some sad falling off. As long as I am mounting the ladder I will hold on."[1]

Gilman was one of many transplanted New Englanders in the thriving seaport of Charleston. A Harvard graduate, he had moved to the city in 1819 to become minister of the Second Independent Church of Charleston, the first Unitarian church to be established in the South. It was a position he would hold for the rest of his life. Gilman was a man of broad abilities with interests in science and philosophy as well as literature. His wife, Caroline, was a poet who had published poems in the fledgling *North American Review*, printed in Boston. The couple befriended Percival and introduced him to the members of their literary society, among them Aaron

Smith Willington, another New Englander, who had established the first newspaper in the city, the *Charleston Courier*.

Never had Percival been among such sympathetic admirers who welcomed him with open arms, delighting in the verse that spontaneously flowed from his pen. One of his admirers was the bookseller William Babcock, who was from New Haven, where his family were booksellers and printers well known for publishing chapbooks and children's books, among them Noah Webster's spellers. Besides going for walks with him, Babcock enthusiastically assisted in the publication of Percival's second book, *Clio I*, in January 1822, only two months after Percival's arrival.[2] However, any admirer of Percival had to be willing to overlook (or make excuses for) his peculiarities, such as his stony interactions with women that led to awkward social situations. Caroline Gilman wrote that although she showed him every courtesy when he visited her home, Percival totally ignored her, talking only to her husband. "Evening after evening passed and he never even glanced my way." Refusing to be slighted, Caroline Gilman invited three beautiful young women to bring their sewing for a social evening at which Percival would be present. There the women sat with thimbles on their fingers as "their needles—the feminine social electric wire—were in motion," according to Gilman. She then presented Percival with Walter Scott's poem "The Lady of the Lake" to read aloud to them as they sewed. He did so reluctantly in a low voice "without any seeming appreciation of the delicate harmony." Yet Gilman noted that Percival was not impervious to the charms of one of the young women, as was made clear in a love poem he subsequently wrote titled "Flower of a Southern Garden," which began, "Flower of a Southern Garden newly blowing, / Fair as a lily bending on its stem, / Whose curled and yellow locks in ringlets flowing, / Need not the lustre of a diadem." Overcome with desire, he wrote that with her by his side, "the hours might flit away so sweetly blest that time would melt into eternity." Yet he never spoke a word to the woman about his passion—the poem was all. While Gilman's attempt to get Percival to socialize with women totally failed, she wrote that she sometimes detected a "furtive smile" on his face and that all the women "felt there was a pearl in the shell we were not allowed to open."[3]

In the preface to *Clio I*, Percival wrote, "Poetry should be a sacred thing, not to be thrown away on the dull and low realities of life. It should live only with those feelings and imaginations, which are above the world, and are the anticipations of a brighter and better being." Poetry should have nothing to do with "defilement or decay." He attempted to hold to that idealistic standard by including poems not only about flowers and lovely young women but also patriotic poems about freedom that looked back nostalgically at the Revolutionary War. He even appended two rambling essays at the end of the book on the nature of magnanimity and the imagination. Yet Percival did not exclude the "low realities of life" or "defilement and decay." One of the most unusual poems in the collection is an untitled soliloquy written in the voice of a young woman whose husband is unfaithful and cruel. It is emotionally dramatic but not mawkish as the woman utters, "I had a husband, once, who loved me—now, . . . ," the carefully placed commas and dash adding a hesitant grief to her words. Many years later, when the poem was included in Percival's collected works, one critic commented, "There is so much dramatic power that we cannot but lament that a mind capable of such refinement of feeling had not oftener ventured on the creation of character."[4]

The reaction to *Clio I* in Charleston and around the country was very positive. Newspaper editors reprinted the unnamed poem, sticking on various titles, such as "The Deserted Wife," "The Neglected Wife," and "The Dissipated Husband," and then signing it with the capital letter *P*. It became one of the most popular poems of the decade, with an editor gushing, "We have often been delighted with the following beautiful effusion of our countryman Dr. Percival, and think it one of the happiest productions of this first of American bards."[5]

Willington also published several of Percival's new poems in the *Charleston Courier*, among them the one widely regarded as his best, "The Coral Grove." Purely descriptive, it is written in third person and reveals Percival's keen ability to observe nature, which does not point to the sublime, as it often does in his other poems, but is sufficient in and of itself. There is neither personal turmoil nor reference to Greek mythology. While floating in a small boat in shallow coastal waters, Percival peers down at the "sand like the mountain drift" and the crimson leaf of the dulse, where "purple mullet and goldfish rove." What he observes is a silent world where a gentle current ripples the seaweed in the same way that a soft wind bends corn in an upland field.[6] In "The Coral Grove," all is calm, beautiful, and safe from surface storms.[7]

Percival was also calm, but not for long. In late March, he abruptly closed his medical office (having seen only one patient) and departed Charleston to the dismay of his new friends, among them Willington, who subsequently wrote with compassionate understanding in the *Charleston Courier* about his leaving:

> Percival, the American poet, who is reaping in the praises of his countrymen throughout the Union the fruits of his genius and the harvest of his hopes left Charleston yesterday in the *Empress* for New York. It is honorable in this country that his talents should be so generally appreciated. He is destined to outlive many generations after this in the annals of men. We, in Charleston, loved him for the artless simplicity, the delicate sensitiveness, the sweet timidity of his spirit and his manner; and we admired the amazing fertility of his mind, always spontaneously pouring forth, as from an exhaustless spring, pure and beautiful and unearthly thoughts. We sympathized with him too, for he was at times melancholy and dejected, as Genius is when it is on the earth.[8]

There were several reasons for Percival's departure. His failure to make a living was one. His opposition to slavery was another, about which he wrote to a friend in the north, "They make a great parade of liberty in the South but it is nothing but the liberty of driving negroes and playing the fool with their earnings."[9] Then, too, he was homesick, writing in the poem "I Would Follow the Sun" that it was pleasant during the cold winter months to be able to wander in a tropical place "where flowers, fruits, and foliage are

FIG. 4.1. Unidentified artist, *James Gates Percival*. Published in *Recollections of a Lifetime* by Samuel Griswold Goodrich, 1856. A friend of Percival, Goodrich wrote in his memoirs that melancholy pervaded Percival's poetry and that there was "a certain wildness in his air and manner."

blended above" and the "wind comes perfumed from the orange and lime." However, with the return of spring to New England, he longed to go home "when the woods are in leaf, and the orchards are blooming." (See plates 11, 12, and 13.) A friend of Percival's wrote, "He never lost his attachment for his birthplace, returning to it at intervals of relaxation from his literary pursuits, and ever regarding it as the dearest place on earth."[10]

Over and above those reasons, there was Percival's perpetual inability to remain on an even mental keel. In his letter to Gilman written from New Haven, Percival apologized for not responding to prior correspondence, "I had besides some of my peculiar indisposition about me, and the result was one of those dark and blue compounds of feeling that always make me my own worst enemy." To prove that he was doing better and that he was serious about his declaration of "I think therefore I am" reconceived as "I write therefore I am," Percival let Gilman know that he was working on a second canto to "Prometheus." In fact, he had written nine stanzas since breakfast. Unfortunately, such productivity was not a sign of mental health but of mania; the second canto of "Prometheus" was 1,908 lines long, the first canto (begun while Percival was at Yale) was 1,458 lines long, for a total of 3,366 lines divided into 374 stanzas. Some of Percival's best writing is in "Prometheus," but also some of the most overwrought.[11]

Despite Percival's poetic *gloom* and *doom* (words that appear along with *tomb* in the first stanza of "Prometheus"), to his friends in New Haven it appeared that his brief sojourn in Charleston had mellowed him. As William Chauncey Fowler, Percival's former classmate, put it, "the ice seemed to have been melted out of him in that genial climate." To Fowler's surprise, Percival even made friends with a circle of "intelligent and refined ladies" in New Haven, with whom "he talked about aesthetics, whether in their application to nature or moral sentiment, or human conduct; or he strolled with them occasionally in the field, surveying such objects on the earth or in the sky as would interest a naturalist, or a poet."[12]

Percival chose the title *Clio*, which he bestowed on three books (differentiated by volume number), because Clio was the Greek muse of history and lyre playing and was often portrayed carrying a scroll or tablet.[13] Percival tended to see the world of ancient Greece as superior to the Christian world that replaced it, even though he professed a rarified faith in the latter. He yearned to dwell in that long-gone time of enchantment when every grove had its sacred spirit, every brook its nymph, and every dark cave had within it a sibyl intoning mysterious words.[14] Percival's chief form of worship was poetry, which he described as "a holy and in-spired delirium," indicating that he may have believed that the glorious spirits "of loveliness and light" that visited him were real, describing them in one poem as "substantial essences, pure forms, that had a look and voice."[15]

Both *Clio I* and *II* received good reviews, including a strong one in the *North American Review* by Samuel Gilman, who wrote, "We regard his powers and resources as inexhaustible." However, the praise did not result in increased book sales. The writer of an arti-cle in the *New York Mirror* pointed out one of the barriers to finan-cial success, noting that while Percival was in Charleston several poems appeared under the signature of *P* in the city's newspaper "whence they were copied throughout the United States, on ac-count of their uncommon intrinsic excellence, without it being known by whom they had been written."[16] The republishing of po-ems in newspapers and magazines around the country without a poet's knowledge, consent, or payment was commonplace. For Per-cival, it helped to build his fame a little, that is, if readers could figure out whom the letter *P* stood for, but it did not bring him any money.

Percival was not paid by the publishers of his books, instead financing their publication by the common practice of subscrip-tion, in which people paid in advance for a copy, which meant a poet had to market the book to cover the cost of production before it went to booksellers. This practice angered Percival, who com-plained bitterly to a friend about having to make an unfavorable contract with a bookseller. "I made the contract with him because I owed him one hundred and fifty dollars for the last part of *Pro-metheus*. Perhaps sixty or seventy copies of that book have been sold though I doubt whether fifty have been retailed." In the same letter he decried the poor treatment not only of poets but also of artists, mentioning his friend Samuel Morse, who had spent a year and a half in Washington D.C. painting the monumental (87 × 131 inches) *House of Representatives*, only to have to pay out of his own pocket to have it exhibited in New York City. Percival complained, "Who would write or paint any good thing for such a *fashionable vulgar* as ours?"[17]

Percival published *Clio III* in 1827, but it also failed to sell, eliciting a review in the *American Quarterly Review* that damned with faint praise all of Percival's poetry: "Unlike the poets of highest renown, Mr. Percival holds more intercourse with nature than with his own race. The clouds, the mountains, and the ever-changing and yet eternal beauties of the earth, are his delight. His Muse meditates in loneliness. He tells us more of his own sensations when his mind is wrought upon by poetic excitement than of the sympathies of others. It is a metaphysical passion for nature; a sublime and self-denying and almost misanthropic spirit of meditation; an indifference to the great mass of men that we most frequently meet in his poetry."[18]

If there was a high point in Percival's career, it occurred in 1828 when the *New York Mirror* printed a full-page engraving of nine "Eminent Living American Poets." Percival was in the center encircled by smaller engravings of the other poets, including William Cullen Bryant, Fitz-Green Halleck, and Samuel Woodworth, whose sentimental poem "The Old Oaken Bucket" was very popular throughout the nation.[19] To heighten the engraving's visual effect, the artist had drawn an eagle with wings outstretched at the top and then had entwined the portraits with tendrils, laurel wreaths, and bunting as if the poets were conquering heroes.

Another sign of success was that Percival's poems began appearing in anthologies, such as *Specimens of American Poetry* and *The Poets and Poetry of America*, a copy of which was in the library of the Dickinson family in Amherst, where it was read by Emily, then in her teens. They also appeared in versions of *McGuffey's Reader*, introducing Percival to generations of young readers, who memorized "The Eagle" and then stood up and declaimed nervously in front of their classmates and doting parents the words "Bird of the broad and sweeping wing! Thy home is high in heaven." In 1830, the poet John Greenleaf Whittier, then twenty-three years old, declared, "We pity the man who does not love the poetry of Percival."[20]

Percival's relationships with poets, writers, and editors were often prickly and competitive. For example, his old friend, Samuel Griswold Goodrich, introduced him to James Fenimore Cooper in

FIG. 4.2. Unidentified artist, *Eminent Living American Poets*. Engraving published in the *New York Mirror*, January 1828. Considered by many critics to be the best poet of the age, Percival was depicted in the center of this engraving surrounded by eight poets, among them William Cullen Bryant.

New York City, where Percival lived for a very brief time. "It is not easy to conceive of two persons more strongly contrasting each other," Goodrich wrote. "Mr. Cooper was in person solid, robust, athletic . . . Percival, on the contrary, was tall and thin, his chest sunken, his limbs long and feeble. . . . Yet these two men conversed pleasantly together. After a time Percival was drawn out, and the stores of his mind were poured forth as from a cornucopia. I could see Cooper's grey eyes dilate with delight and surprise." Subsequently, Cooper helped Goodrich obtain a book contract for Percival. However, Percival did not hold the same high opinion of Cooper, describing him in a letter to a friend as "a literary parasite" whose fictional characters, such as Natty Bumppo, were beneath contempt: "I sometimes feel bitter towards a public that can encourage such stuff as *The Pioneers*, or at least the great mass of it and leave authors of real merit unrewarded."[21]

Edgar Allan Poe may have used Percival as his model for Roderick Usher, the main character in the story "The Fall of the House of Usher," published in 1839. Poe, who knew well the terrors of mental illness, described Usher as a morbidly sensitive and deeply depressed recluse. When the story's unnamed narrator arrives at the gothic mansion to visit Usher, he is dismayed by his old friend's transmogrification: "The horrible white of his skin and the strange light in his eyes surprised me and even made me afraid. His hair had been allowed to grow, and in its softness, it did not fall around his face but seemed to lie upon the air. I could not even with an effort, see in my friend, the appearance of a simple human being."[22]

William Cullen Bryant loved "the reckless intoxication" of Percival's poetry, the recklessness being related to Percival's penchant for writing fast and not revising—as indicated by his comment to Gilman that he had written nine stanzas of "Prometheus" since breakfast. Percival, who was close in age and background to Bryant but very different in temperament, was undoubtedly pleased with Bryant's assessment. He himself claimed that he disliked poetry that "bears the marks of the file and the burnisher." Poetry needed "something savage and luxuriant." Unfortunately, later assessments of Percival's poetry were that writing speed and lack of revision were the main reasons for his ultimate failure as a poet, resulting in sloppy and unfocused poems, some of which were far too long, the prime example being "Prometheus," which didn't exactly end but petered out in exhaustion.[23]

In the many newspaper and magazine articles about Percival during this period, the journalists frequently found it impossible to gauge his poetry separately from his peculiar life (which provided great fodder for gossip) and dramatic personal appearance. Even his friends could not make the separation. Nathaniel Parker Willis, who knew Percival well, wrote in the July 1830 issue of the *American Monthly Magazine*, "The most legitimate poet—the most authentic child of the Muses, baptized and cradled undeniably by our deserted well—is Percival. It is written broad on his forehead. He is the only poet in the land who looks like one."[24] Willis had in mind Lord Byron, who was dashing, disillusioned, and moody. Even their poems bore a resemblance.[25] As Byron's fame began to decline, so also did Percival's. When, in 1831, Percival placed an announcement in the *New York Mirror* to solicit subscribers to fund a new volume of poetry, the effort failed miserably even with the help of friends and family.[26] Twelve years would pass before Percival would publish another book, *The Dream of a Day*, which was doomed to oblivion before the ink dried. Goodrich was convinced that Percival's identification with Byron brought about his downfall: "I think he had been deeply injured—nay ruined—by the reading of Byron's works, at that precise age when his soul was in all the sensitive bloom of spring, and its killing frost of atheism, of misanthropy, of pride, and scorn, fell upon it, and converted it into a scene of desolation." However, it must also be pointed out that the same obscurity would fall on almost all of the poets of the era. Of the poets pictured in the engraving *Eminent Living American Poets*, only William Cullen Bryant would achieve any lasting fame, as would Washington Irving, who, however, was not a poet.[27]

Percival's immediate problem was not his declining reputation but the lack of a paying job, made worse by his insatiable need to buy books, running up a hefty tab at Howe's bookstore in New Haven. From 1822 through the early 1830s, Percival took various editorial positions to make ends meet, including a brief stint as a newspaper editor in New Haven. Through Dr. George Hayward in

Boston, he received a contract from the publisher Samuel Walker to work as an editor on Vicesimus Knox's multivolume work *Elegant Extracts: Being a Copious Selection of Instructive, Moral and Entertaining Passages from the Most Eminent British Poets.*[28]

By far the most unusual editorial job was his work with Noah Webster, then sixty-nine years old. In 1827, Sherman Converse, a publisher and editor of the *Connecticut Journal* in New Haven, approached Percival about reading a proof of *An American Dictionary of the English Language*, which Webster had been working on for about twenty-five years and which Converse was preparing for publication. With seventy thousand words, the dictionary was proving to be a challenge for Converse, who badly needed help. On the surface, Percival was a good choice because he was fluent in many languages, was knowledgeable in the new field of etymology, and knew scientific terminology. Percival accepted the task but immediately locked horns with Webster, who could be demanding, as the following exchange makes clear: "I have to request you not to write on the MSS," wrote Webster truculently, "as many of your remarks are illegible and they injure the writing, which is already bad enough. You will oblige me to write all your remarks . . . on a separate piece of paper." Percival shot back, "If you have confidence in me, my articles had better remain as they are. If you have not, it is idle for me to have any further connection with the dictionary." They made a token peace and Percival continued on, taking too much time and complaining about the poor pay but doing a good job nonetheless. Charles Shepard wrote that Percival "translated and revised so carefully, he corrected so many errors and added so many foot-notes, that his industry actually devoured his own wages; and his eight dollars gradually diminished to a diurnal fifty cents." And yet for all his complaining, Percival remarked to a friend, "I took much pleasure in editing Webster's Dictionary than in anything else I have done." It was published in 1828 without Percival's name appearing on the frontispiece.[29]

Percival's editorial work helped him cover living expenses, but he continued to believe that his true calling was as a poet. At the same time, a sea change was occurring in American culture that made his chances of success even less likely. The decade of the 1820s had been marked by nostalgia for the past and uncertainty for the future. With the passing of the last of the Revolutionary War generation—Thomas Jefferson and John Adams had died on the same day, July 4, 1826—there was a sense that the country's finest hour had already gone by and that the nation had fallen away from its Arcadian ideals. Percival expressed that sense in "Prometheus":

> This is the old age of our fallen race;
> We mince in steps correct, but feeble; creep
> By rule unwavering in a tortoise pace;
> We do not, like the new-born ancient, leap
> At once o'er mind's old barriers, but we keep
> Drilling and shaving down the wall; we play
> With stones and shells and flowers; and as we peep
> In nature's outward folds, like infants, say,
> How bright and clear and pure our intellectual day.[30]

This sense of the passing of an age was also conveyed by other writers and artists in the period from 1820 to the mid-1830s, including James Fenimore Cooper in *The Last of the Mohicans* and Thomas Cole in his allegorical series of paintings titled *The Course of Empire*, the first painting being *The Savage State*, followed by *The Pastoral State*, *Consummation*, *Destruction*, and finally *Desolation*, in which everything that had been achieved by civilization is ruined. At the same time, there was the stirring of a new vision. The nation was vast and its land was *almost* overpowering in grandeur, but not quite. The white man's destiny was to conquer it even if it took another Promethean seizure of fire to do so. It was the coming of the steam engine that would be the essence of that new fiery power.[31]

By 1830, the potential of steam power was obvious to everyone. In his aptly named book about this era, *The Machine in the Garden: Technology and the Pastoral Ideal in America*, Leo Marx analyzed the longing for the bucolic past that was counterbalanced by excitement for the industrial future. The metaphor of the machine in the garden summed up the contradiction at the heart of the national identity. "In newspapers, popular magazines, and political speeches of the era, the new technological artifacts won praise as emblems of the 'conquest of nature,' or of America's 'Manifest Destiny' to occupy the continent, or—most often and fulsomely—of the prevailing faith in the idea that history is a record of steady, continuous, cumulative material Progress." There is no better example of this contradiction than occurred in 1833 when Andrew Jackson—a backwoods country boy from the Carolinas—became the first president to ride the "Iron Horse" operated by the Baltimore & Ohio Railroad. The railroad was noisy, dangerous, and destructive of nature—but what power it had! It was a sign of a youthful nation ready to surge forward. And it was unstoppable— if enough iron and coal could be mined to build it and keep it running.[32]

Poetry that had a grandiose or otherworldly quality was outdated. It was Ralph Waldo Emerson who made it clear where poetry was headed: "We have listened too long to the courtly muses of Europe." It was time for the quotidian, for the American, for the un-mythological to be upheld without reference to the great, the remote, and the romantic. "I embrace the common," Emerson proclaimed, "I explore and sit at the feet of the familiar, the low. Give me insight into to-day, and you may have the antique and future worlds." The best exemplar of Emerson's new age of poetry would be Walt Whitman, who wrote of the workday life and restless energy of a diverse America.[33]

In his letter to Samuel Gilman in the early 1820s, Percival had written about his having "two strings to my bow, perhaps twenty, and if one won't shoot, perhaps another will." Poetry was one string, geology was another. It was time to restring his bow. In this respect a comment made by Samuel Griswold Goodrich is significant. Goodrich admitted ruefully in his *Recollections of a Lifetime* that Percival was an enigma to him and that he considered his life to have been "a complete shipwreck." Yet Goodrich saw beyond his own assessment, writing that besides Percival's encyclopedic knowledge and powerful imagination, there was "his powers of combination, his judgment," as exemplified first in his work on Webster's dictionary and second in his "larger and grander surveys of geology—the largest and grandest of practical sciences. Such compass and such precision of knowledge—such power of exact as well as vast combination are indeed marvelous." To Goodrich, it was Percival's monumental work in geology that brought him to his peak.[34]

FIVE

The Shift to Geology

Like a cat, Percival had nine lives. Unlike a cat, he led those lives simultaneously, not sequentially. There had never been a time in all the years Percival was a physician, a poet, and a multilingual editor that he was not also a geologist. In the spring and summer of 1821, he walked across New York State to Niagara Falls, where he was transfixed by the power of the thundering water and rock, writing in a sonnet, "I too have seen thy ever-pouring flood, / Mightiest of cataracts, Niagara! / Have seen thy restless waters rush away, / And on the beetling rock alone have stood."[1]

On his journey he explored the Catskill Mountains and the Finger Lakes, continually writing poetry. In one of his most famous poems, "Seneca Lake," he wrote of his arrival after a very long walk: "One evening in the pleasant month of May / on a green hillock swelling from the shore / above thy emerald wave, when the clear west / was all one sheet of light, I sat me down / wearied yet happy." When he awoke the next morning, having spent the night on the hill lulled to sleep by the sound of frogs and crickets, he discovered to his joy that the lake had been transformed under the influence of a strong breeze. Instead of calm water there were deep-green waves rippling brightly "as if they were worlds of stars, or gems, or crystals."[2]

Percival also made scientific observations that found their way into Silliman's *American Journal of Science and Arts*, to which he was a frequent contributor. To *do* geology was a feat of the imagination as great as to *write* a poem, requiring him to see in his mind's eye mountains worn down to foothills while far below magma seethed. For example, in 1824 he reviewed *An Essay on Salt*, written by Stephen Van Rensselaer, a Harvard graduate and wealthy landowner in the Hudson Valley. Percival began by complimenting Van Rensselaer on his work, but then he pointed out some errors, explaining what he himself had observed about the strata of limestone and sandstone in western New York. He was referring to the same trip that had inspired him to write poetry, but this time his language was purely scientific, stripped of metaphors and similes, of rhythm and rhyme, yet still maintaining a sense of awe for the vastness of time encapsulated in a tiny fossil. "If you cross the country in a line from Seneca Lake to the Catskill Mountains, you find after leaving the limestone a black horizontal argillaceous slate full of small bivalves. This slate forms the shores of Cayuga and Seneca Lakes." Near the headwaters of the Susquehanna River, he discovered that the black slate turned brown and yellow before turning red on approaching the sandstones of the Catskill Mountains, while still further east the limestone abounded "with shells and hornstone." He closed the review on a conciliatory note toward Van Rensselaer, writing, "We offer these remarks only as suggestions, and we should be happy if they might aid any one in arriving at more definite conclusions."[3]

At the same time as his poems were appearing in the influential literary magazine *Knickerbocker*, so also were some thought-provoking essays, among them one titled "The Philosopher," by which Percival meant a scientist. It opens with the description of a scene by a first-person narrator: "I had traveled several hours in a stage, on a cold winter's day, with an individual who had observed an entire silence." The narrator (presumably Percival) then describes the stranger as tall, thin, and conveying a sense of melancholy, in other words, he describes himself. Stopping for the night, the narrator attempts to make small talk with the man, asking about possible causes for the sudden change in the weather. The man replies in a gush of words:

> Our business, as men of science, is not first with causes. We
> must observe and collect facts, compare and arrange them,

and then perhaps we will discover causes. If we do not, a body of facts, methodically arranged, is a science, and as such capable of the most useful application. But our philosophers and men of science, so called, are continually hastening back to first causes. They mistake hypotheses for conclusions and so involve themselves, and all who follow their dicta, in a false light, which is but darkness. . . . Impatience of prolonged research, incapacity for far extended views, and an eagerness to arrive at some final conclusion, however hasty or insufficient, are the prevailing characteristics of minds that pretend to investigate.

The monologue continues until finally the man falls silent and will not say another word—also a trait of Percival's. Were it not for the fictionalized form of "The Philosopher," which provided Percival with a modicum of cover, the essay could be seen as a frontal attack on scientists who pushed their research too fast, were careless about analysis, and jumped to unfounded results. Alluding to geology, the philosopher insists that "a body of facts, methodically arranged" (meaning data in modern usage) was still a useful "science." This essay was published at the time Percival had begun his own "prolonged research" on the geology of Connecticut and was under pressure to get the work done and reach a "final conclusion." He was also chafing against pressure to provide geological evidence that the first cause was a divinely ordained flood.[4]

Percival's reviews of scientific papers by Europeans meant that he was up-to-date on what was happening in several fields, among them the new discipline of paleontology, which was beginning to undermine the idea of a single worldwide flood. In 1824, he reviewed in detail a paper on the classification of fossilized plants by the French botanist Adolphe-Thèodore Brongniart (1801–1876), a young protégé of Georges Cuvier (1769–1832). Paleontology was quickly becoming of great importance to geology because the study of the different types of fossils found in sedimentary rock held the key to determining the age of that rock. For example, if a geologist found two sedimentary rocks that he suspected were of the same age but that looked different, he could examine the fossils found in each. If the fossils were similar, then so was the age of the rocks; if not, then the rocks were formed at different times. To reach that level of understanding, meticulous comparison of fossils with living species was essential, and then that information had to be classified in such a way that other scientists could apply it with accuracy in their own work, which is why Brongniart's research was important. Percival also reviewed scientific papers on the geology of Sicily, famous for its active volcano, Mount Etna. Fluent in French, German, and Italian, Percival read these papers in their original languages before they were translated (often by him) and made available to other geologists in the United States, putting him at the leading edge of his field.[5]

One of Percival's largest undertakings was his translation of *A System of Universal Geography*, a mammoth six-volume work by Malte-Brun (1775–1826), a Danish-French scientist.[6] At that time geography and geology were closely related. The height of the Swiss Alps, the direction of the rivers in Africa, the latitude and longitude of volcanoes in South America—this geographical information was essential to geologists. Not long after Malte-Brun's death in 1826, Percival signed a contract with the publishing firm Samuel Walker in Boston to edit the work, but he found the translation from French to English to be so bad he was forced to retranslate. Despite an acrimonious relationship with the printer over the amount of time he was taking, Percival completed the task and the English version of *A System of Universal Geography* was published in 1834.[7]

Charles Upham Shepard, a Yale professor who worked closely with Percival on the survey of Connecticut, was astounded by Percival's voluminous knowledge of geography. "Far from confining it to the names and boundaries of countries, seas, and lakes, to the courses of rivers and the altitudes of mountains," Shepard wrote, "he connected it with meteorology, natural history, and the leading facts of human history, ethnology, and archaeology. He knew London as thoroughly as most Americans know New York or Philadelphia, and yet he had never crossed the Atlantic." Further evidence of the extent of Percival's knowledge is found in his review of Van Rensselaer's *An Essay on Salt*, in which Percival discussed traprock in the Rocky Mountains as well as in India, where the "most extensive trap formations in the world" spread out uniformly over a vast area. There was nothing unusual about a person being widely read in geography; what set Percival apart was his total recall.[8]

Even when Percival was employed in an editorial capacity with no link to geology, the subject still came to the fore. In 1823, while serving briefly as editor of the newspaper *Connecticut Herald*, he wrote an editorial in favor of the digging of the Farmington Canal, expressing the belief that canals, such as the recently completed Erie Canal, were superior to rivers for commercial transport because their depth was uniform, horse power could be used, and the flow of water could be controlled. The proposed route of the canal was from New Haven to Northampton to the west of the traprock ridges. Percival described the type of soil along the route as "easily excavated," but because the sandstone in the area was subject to erosion, he recommended that traprock or gneiss be used for construction instead, pointing out that an abundant supply of both was "within no great distance." Knowing that the financial backers of the plan wanted nothing less than to shift the geo-economic balance to New Haven and away from Hartford (which had long benefitted from trade on the Connecticut River), Percival suggested that a fair solution would be to dig a connector from the main canal through Meriden and Berlin to the Connecticut River. Unfortunately, his suggestions were ignored. The canal was dug to the west without any connection to the river, and as he had predicted the banks were subject to frequent collapse.[9]

Whenever Percival returned to Kensington, his long, solitary walks were not given over to daydreaming but to searching for minerals and rocks, always on the lookout for a glint on the ground or a colored vein in the cliff face. Such sharp observation led to the publication of at least two articles; one was on a lead mine not far from his home, which had provided lead for bullets during the Revolutionary War; the other was on "sulphate of barites" that he had found in a vein in the nearby traprock ridge, remarking that the surrounding area was part of the red sandstone formation that extended up and down the valley.[10]

As a boy, Edward Robbins, the son of the minister Royal Robbins, remembered meeting Percival on one of his geological walks and was surprised by his appearance, which was appropriate for a geologist but not for a poet. "It was on one of those expeditions, that the writer well remembered seeing him clad in an old frock coat, buttoned up to the chin; on his head was a straw hat which looked as if it had been tanned by exposure to the storms of a century, furrowed with seams, and somewhat coarse for wear; the rest of his apparel beneath appeared to consist of a rough, coarse pair of pantaloons and boots of a similar quality; while from his pocket projected the handle of a hammer."[11]

By 1830, little had changed in the debate between the Neptunists and the Plutonists. Werner's ideas on water were still ascendant. Hutton's ideas about a uniform geological process and that the earth had a molten interior had yet to be widely accepted. Percival's study of the traprock made him a Plutonist. However, he did not use that term, nor did he dismiss the immense role of water. Silliman was still a Neptunist, even though he believed that traprock was igneous. Yet solid research not just in paleontology but also in crystallography was beginning to affect the thinking of all geologists, no matter whether their allegiance was to Werner or Hutton. Crystallography was developed by Rene Just Haüy (1743–1822), a French priest and mineralogist who applied mathematics to the study of crystals, such as tourmaline and topaz, devising a system of identification and classification that was proving to be a powerful tool in the hands of geologists.[12]

As a result of these advances, Silliman began to vacillate on the age of the earth being six thousand years old, proposing cautiously (as did many other geologists) that each day of creation was far longer than twenty-four hours, the word for *day* in Hebrew meaning an undefined period of time. To Silliman, Christians need not feel threatened by the lengthening of creation. With a little sleight of hand, the new geological findings could be made to fit with the Biblical account. In 1829, Silliman had even chosen as a textbook for his students *Introduction to Geology* by the Englishman Robert Bakewell, a follower of Hutton, but then he added a section on his own Wernerian views. He renamed the compilation *Outline of the*

FIG. 5.1. Unidentified artist, *Junction of Trap Rock and Sandstone at Rocky Hill,* published in *American Journal of Science,* 1830. When the famous Scottish geologist Charles Lyell visited Connecticut, Silliman and Percival took him to see the traprock. Barber copied this lithograph published in the *American Journal of Science* and included it his *Connecticut Historical Collections.*

Course of Geological Lectures Given In Yale College. By presenting his students with both points of view, he hoped to encourage them to think for themselves. However, if he thought that most of his students would become Neptunists, he was destined for disappointment. The change was in the other direction: Silliman discretely moved toward adopting Hutton's ideas about the earth's internal heat, even admitting that igneous traprock was formed by magma far below the earth's crust pushing up through fractures.[13]

Geology was about to get a boost of energy that would increase its popularity and its influence. Between 1830 and 1833, the Scottish geologist Charles Lyell (1797–1875) published his three-volume work, *Principles of Geology,* that would have a major impact in the United States by bringing some of Hutton's ideas into sharper focus. *Principles* was an attempt to summarize the field while providing a push in a new direction. Lyell picked the word *Principles* to acknowledge Isaac Newton's *Principia* and to imply that his work was also of the highest order of magnitude. Lyell was nothing if not ambitious, fashioning himself a "geological logician" who, like Newton, upheld scientific methods.[14] It was not that Lyell was always right, in fact he was very wrong on many points. However, he presented the work in a comprehensive and readable fashion, which extended its reach to an audience far larger than the small cadre of geologists. Lyell began *Principles* by reaching back to the Hindus, the Egyptians, and the Greeks, exploring their ideas of cyclical creation and destruction across monumental time scales. Mountains rose up and wore away. Plants and animals died and were pressed down into mud, leaving behind fossils in strata that were like the pages of a decipherable book.

One of Lyell's purposes was to bring clarity to the meaning of geology. According to Mott Greene in his book *Geology in the Nineteenth Century*, "Properly understood and practiced, geology was to be the application of the sciences of chemistry, natural philosophy, mineralogy, zoology, comparative anatomy, and botany to the elucidation of the history of the earth." Geology was not a subdivision of mineralogy or cosmology. "Lyell wished to avoid both myopic and gratuitous hypotheses by finding for geology a middle ground—more than a study of rocks and minerals, less than a theory of the origin of the globe (or universe)."[15]

Both Silliman and Percival read Lyell's work as soon as it appeared and over the next decade corresponded with him. When Lyell visited New Haven in 1841, Silliman and Percival took him on a tour of a quarry in Rocky Hill where strata of traprock and red sandstone could be seen. He also toured East Rock and West Rock, which reminded him of the Salisbury Crags in Edinburgh— the same observation Silliman had made thirty-five years before when in Scotland. In his travel journal, Lyell wrote, "Mr. Percival has shown that they are in reality intrusive and alter the strata in contact both above and below."[16] The alteration was created by the contact of the hot magma rising up through cold sedimentary rock. In turn, this indicated that the sedimentary rock was older than the traprock. Just as fossils could be used as a marker for age, so also could alterations. Since his graduation speech at Yale on the capacity of a genius to move beyond the particular to the universal, Percival had been a thinker about systems, never more so than in geology. It was this that Lyell tacitly acknowledged in his brief journal entry about Percival.

Charles Darwin (1809–1882) also read *Principles*, carrying a copy with him as he traveled as a geologist on the HMS *Beagle* in 1831. The book was important to him because of the idea of deep time. In fact, Darwin felt so indebted to Lyell that he wrote in his book *On the Origin of Species*, "He who can read Sir Charles Lyell's grand work on the Principles of Geology, which the future historian will recognize as having produced a revolution in natural sciences, yet does not admit how incomprehensibly vast have been the past periods of time, may at once close this volume."[17]

One of Lyell's dictates in *Principles* was that geologists should not speculate but seek the true cause of geology based on evidence. However, given that so much of geology was unobservable, it was virtually impossible not to speculate. At the very least, geologists had to extrapolate from partial and conflicting data to answer questions such as, What happened to outcrops on the shoreline that angled down into the sea? There was no way to know. Even Lyell, for all his insistence on nothing-but-the-facts, could not help himself from speculating about the causes of earthquakes and volcanoes, wondering whether they were caused by cavities in the earth's floating crust through which seawater leaked, leading to major disturbances.[18]

At the same time as *Principles* was increasing the popularity of geology, the demand for coal, iron, and many other ores and minerals was growing rapidly in the United States. Politicians and businessmen wanted to know where they could be located and in what quantity; they didn't care whether they were created by flood or fire, six thousand years ago or six million years ago. Their practical approach was to conduct statewide surveys. Already some local surveys had been conducted, such as the one commissioned by Stephen Van Rensselaer of the area around Albany in New York State. It was done by Amos Eaton, who had studied under Silliman

FIG. 5.2. Unidentified artist, *Edward Hitchcock*. Published in *A History of Amherst College During the Administration of its Five Presidents* by William S. Taylor, 1873. Edward Hitchcock was a minister, geologist, and a professor at Amherst, becoming president of the college in 1845. Believing in the Biblical creation story, he tried to reconcile religion and science.

and was a professor at Williams College. Yet no one had conducted a comprehensive large-scale survey in which all the geological resources of a single state were identified. It was one of those bright ideas that is simple enough on paper but is of enormous difficulty to achieve. That difficulty was further increased by the necessity to strike a balance between the scientific objectives of the geologists and the economic objectives of the legislators who held the purse strings.

The first state survey was conducted in Massachusetts by Edward Hitchcock, a professor of geology and moral theology at Amherst College. An ordained minister, he believed in the harmony of science and the Bible.[19] To the public he was best known for proposing that the dinosaur tracks found in Hadley, Massachusetts, in 1802 were made by a large running ground bird that had gone extinct, an idea that presented him with a theological conundrum given that all species were supposed to have been preserved on Noah's ark. However, Hitchcock was a conscientious scientist who endeavored not to reject evidence that ran counter to his religious beliefs. That conscientiousness also marked his geological report and his later efforts to encourage geologists to meet together and share their findings, thereby amicably advancing the science. Begun in 1831 and published in 1832, his report served as the spur for the many surveys that followed, among them Tennessee in 1831; Maryland in 1834; and New Jersey, Virginia, and Connecticut in 1835, although the Connecticut report was not published until 1842. Part of Hitchcock's report was later turned into a guidebook to what he dubbed "scenographical geology" to encourage "gentlemen of taste, intelligence, and leisure . . . to climb our own mountains, and traverse our own deep glens and gorges, where they will find unsophisticated nature, with the dress given them by their Creator, scarcely marred by the hand of man."[20]

Just as geologists made the surveys, so too the surveys made the geologists. Rarely did they have an opportunity to study geology in a comprehensive way totally in the field, giving them a sense of the whole picture. The men who undertook the work were uneven in their knowledge but dedicated in their resolve even though the pay was usually very poor, often not much more than living expenses. In a speech delivered in 1899, John James Stevenson, president of the Geological Society of America, looked back on the beginning of the state surveys and concluded, "Though wholly self-taught, working the country sparsely settled without barometers, without railroad cuts, oil borings, mine shafts, or any of the helps so necessary for us, those men had elaborated systems, had made broad generalizations, had learned much respecting the succession of life." Stevenson was wrong in his claim that all the geologists doing the surveys were self-taught. Several were highly educated, among them the brothers Henry and William Rogers, who conducted surveys in Virginia, New Jersey, and Pennsylvania and who studied the Appalachian Mountains in detail. However, Stevenson was right about the difficulties, the largest being one he failed to mention: geology did not conform to state lines, so while legislators were only interested in what might be of economic value in their state, the mountains and mineral deposits paid no attention.[21]

SIX

The Connecticut Geological Survey

In 1835, Governor Henry Edwards wrote in his annual message to the Connecticut state legislature: "The mineralogical treasures which have been developed within a few years and which are constantly coming to light in different parts of our country, give us reason to believe that we have not as yet availed ourselves to the extent that we might of this source of wealth, and suggest the expediency of a more systematic examination than has hitherto taken place." Edwards was responding to the increasing demand for iron ore and coal to build steam engines and railroads. Iron bog ore, which occurs naturally and is easily accessible, had been used from ancient times up through the colonial era. Rusty-brown in color, it was gathered from swamps fed by iron-rich springs and was used for making numerous items needed by an agrarian and seafaring economy, including ship anchors, cladding, horseshoes, hinges, nails, wheel rims, and tools of all shapes and sizes. However, there was not enough bog ore to meet the needs of large-scale manufacturing.[1]

Since the 1730s iron ore had been quarried in the Salisbury area, but there was uncertainty about the remaining quantity and quality, the difficulty of extraction, and the cost of shipping it to market by teams of oxen. Nor could charcoal, made by burning hard wood under low oxygen conditions, meet the insatiable demands of blast furnaces, of which there were eleven in Connecticut in 1837, making six thousand tons of pig iron a year. Already the hills in the northwest corner of the state where most of the blast furnaces were located were largely denuded of wood.

Governor Edwards did not want Connecticut to be left behind while states such as Pennsylvania and New Jersey literally forged ahead into the front lines of the industrial revolution. During the eighteenth century, Connecticut had been a leader in copper production until the mine in East Granby had played out. In the waste-not-want-not category of Yankee thriftiness, the useless mine was turned into a formidable underground prison in 1773 and named after the infamous Newgate Prison in England. During Edwards's tenure, first as a legislator and then as governor, the prison was closed and the mine was reactivated although the prospects were not promising. On the other hand, brownstone quarrying in Chatham (now Portland) on the Connecticut River was a profitable operation, with the soft reddish-brown rock being used primarily for buildings. There were many small quarries scattered throughout the state, but most of them were worked by farmers who found pickaxing outcroppings on their land to be a profitable off-season sideline to agriculture. None of these quarries was capable of providing a lift to the economy.[2]

Following the lead of the State of Massachusetts, which had hired Edward Hitchcock to conduct its survey, Governor Edwards considered a geological survey of Connecticut to be essential. In addition, he wanted a map drawn to help determine the best routes for railroads and canals. The Farmington Canal had just been completed but not without many construction problems that could have been avoided. In the hope that the survey and map would facilitate future development, Edwards asked Percival to undertake the dual task. Declining the offer because of his literary commitments, Percival recommended Benjamin Silliman. When Silliman also declined, Percival approached Charles Upham Shepard, a professor of mineralogy at Yale, on the governor's behalf. Shepard agreed to do the mineralogy component but only if Percival did the geology component. Otherwise, it was out of the question. Percival agreed.[3]

Shepard's task was much easier than Percival's because mineralogy was well established and the locations of the mines and

FIG. 6.1. John Warner Barber, *Cat Hole Pass*. Engraving with ink wash, published in *Connecticut Historical Collections*, 1836. At the time John Warner Barber drew Cat Hole Pass, between South Mountain and Cat Hole Mountain, it was so narrow in places there was "barely room for a path." He included the rock outcropping resembling the face of George Washington.

quarries in the state were known and could be reached by carriage. When Percival and Shepard looked at a sample of cobalt ore from a mine in Chatham, they knew exactly what it was and its industrial and economic value. They were even aware of its dangers due to its natural occurrence with toxic arsenic ore. When they visited the Newgate copper mine, then owned and operated by the Phenix Mining Company, they could descend by ladder into the shafts— the last prisoners having been moved to an above-ground prison in Wethersfield eight years before.

Percival's task was far more challenging. In fact, at the beginning he himself barely discerned its scope. From sparse and often conflicting evidence, he had to determine what was below ground as indicated by what was above ground. Much of the bedrock was buried under what he called diluvium, meaning soil deposited by a great flood. None of the tools of modern geology were available to him. All he had was a hammer, chisel, shovel, and a magnifying glass. Yet in the long run, Percival's work would have more significance than Shepard's because it indicated where ore was likely to be found, whereas Shepard's work merely indicated where ore was already known to be.

Despite the challenges they faced, there was one factor that made their job much easier than it would have been a hundred years later—almost 75 percent of the state was deforested for agriculture, exposing much of the earth's surface. In *The American Gazetteer* published in 1804, Jedidiah Morse wrote, "The whole state resembles a well cultivated garden." That statement was more applicable to the Connecticut Valley, which was flat and friendly to the plow, than to the rugged and stony uplands, yet even there deforestation was extensive. Because the views from high places were not obscured by vegetation, Percival could accurately map the terrain by tracing the flow of streams and rivers and the alignment of valleys and hills. In the report, Percival gave an example of how outcroppings appeared and disappeared and how it was possible to follow them: "In passing through the village of Wallingford, the range is concealed by diluvium, but has been exposed by excavation. It re-appears near the N.E. part of the village, and further N. in a sandstone ridge, East of the road from Wallingford to the pass at Black Pond, whence it bends abruptly East to Hill's Factory, where it crosses a stream (Wharton's Brook) in a remarkable dike, bordered by green indurated sandstone."[4]

To get a sense of what the land looked like when Percival and Shepard trekked through it, it is helpful to turn to the drawings and engravings by John Warner Barber. Two-and-a-half years younger than Percival, Barber was born in Windsor, Connecticut, and had trained as an engraver. Beginning in 1834, Barber drove around the state in a horse and buggy visiting nearly all the towns, sketching the churches, mills, and homes. From the sketches, he then made ink washes and relief woodcuts. In 1836, he published the engravings in *The Connecticut Historical Collections*. The book sold very well because most people had never traveled far from their homes, so it provided them the opportunity to see what all

FIG. 6.2. John Warner Barber, *Cotton Factory village, Glastenbury.*
Engraving with ink wash, published in *Connecticut Historical Collection,*
1836. When Percival visited Cotton Hollow in Glastonbury (then
spelled with an *e*), the ravine had been cleared of trees and two dams
had been built to harness the power of Roaring Brook for the mills.

the towns in the state looked like. What they discovered was great
homogeneity. Everywhere there were churches with steeples, clap-
boarded homes, mills built of brick and stone, and endless farm
fields enclosed with rail fences or stonewalls. Barber's engravings
gave the impression that Connecticut was bucolic, not wild. Even
when the traprock was pictured it functioned as a backdrop to a
civilized landscape in which most of the trees had been cut down.
The cougar, bear, and wolf had been replaced by the cow, sheep,
and farm dog. For example, the engraving of Meriden shows three
churches, a tavern, and a stagecoach pulled by four horses on the
main road with the traprock ridge rising placidly in the distance.
Another shows Cathole Pass with its profile of a stony face jutting
from the cliff, a natural formation that reminded patriotic citizens
of George Washington.[5]

Barber's engraving of Cotton Hollow in South Glastonbury is
also noteworthy. Now a tree-covered nature preserve, in Barber's

time it was a steep barren ravine through which Roaring Brook gushed. In his engraving, the brook is lined with mill houses, a woolen mill, and the cotton mill from which the hollow took its name. To provide more power to turn the water wheels, two dams had been built across the ravine, one of which is shown. While Barber sketched in a few dead trees clinging to the sides of the ravine, only in the foreground did he place trees with foliage as if to frame the scene, noting on the bottom of his sketch that the trees were buttonwood interspersed with hemlock. Barber also included figures of men in top hats and women in bonnets strolling along the road to the mills while children play in an open space by the houses. This totally exposed view of Cotton Hollow is the one that Percival saw, enabling him to recognize at a glance the lay of the land and the type of rock.[6]

Shepard and Percival began traveling by horse and carriage in July 1835 and concluded in October for the year. They resumed their work in the spring of 1836, visiting nearly every town and surveying the entire state. Years later, Shepard recounted vivid memories of traveling with Percival, whom he found to be peculiar but not without personal warmth, even showing on occasion a sense of humor. As they traveled together through the rural areas, "great was the wonder" at their carriage loaded with the tools of the geologic trade, making it necessary for them to explain what they were doing, particularly since they were crossing private property—digging soil here, chipping rock there. Shepard wrote in the preface to his report that he and Percival had found a great lack of knowledge about mineralogy among the inhabitants. "Many persons, not otherwise wanting in intelligence, were met with, whose belief in the virtues of the divining rod were unshaken, iron-pyrite was often explored for gold, talcy rocks were ground for plaster, and plumbaginous mica-slate extensively mined for coal." Shepard didn't mind explaining what their work entailed, but Percival found such conversations to be a trial even though most people were interested and accepting. According to Shepard, there was one humorous exception:

In New Milford, an inquisitive farmer requested us, in a somewhat ungracious manner, to give an account of ourselves. Percival replied that we were acting under a commission from the Governor to ascertain the useful minerals of the State; whereupon our utilitarian friend immediately demanded to be informed how the citizens at large, including himself, were to be benefited by the undertaking—putting question on question in a fashion which was most pertinacious and almost impertinent. Percival became impatient, and tried to hurry away. "I demand the information," exclaimed the New-Milfordite; "I demand it as my right. You are only servants of the people; and you are paid, in part at least, out of my pocket." "I'll tell you what we'll do," said Percival; "We can't stop, but we'll refund. Your portion of the geological tax—let me see—it must be about two cents. We prefer handing you this to encountering a further delay." Our agricultural friend and master did not take the money, although he did take the hint, and in sulky silence withdrew from our company.[7]

Occasionally farmers thought Shepard and Percival were vagabonds who were looking for work. One politely suggested they seek employment in a nearby mill. Once, when traveling through Lebanon, they were threatened by a madman. Because he was digging up cobblestones by the road and smashing them with an axe, Percival and Shepard thought at first that he was a "brother geologist" until he approached menacingly with the axe in one hand and half a brick in the other. He began to rave about boxes of jewels that belonged to King Jerome, who he claimed was the king of the world. As he advanced toward them, they spurred their horses and bolted away before he attacked. The reverse situation also occurred, with Percival himself being suspected of insanity when he was traveling alone without the ameliorating influence of Shepard. Once an innkeeper saw Percival picking up rocks and asked him what he was doing, but Percival would not give him an explanation. Thinking he might be a horse thief, the innkeeper held him surreptitiously with the help of the neighbors. Luckily a doctor who knew Percival

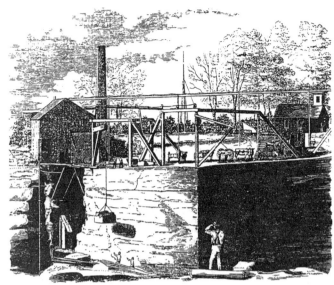

MIDDLESEX QUARRY.

FIG. 6.3. Unidentified artist, *Quarry belonging to the Middle-sex Company*. Lithograph published in *The National Magazine*, vol. III, no. 4. To conduct the geological survey of Connecticut, Percival and Charles Upham Shepard, a professor of mineralogy at Yale, visited mines and quarries, providing a rare opportunity to see below the earth's surface.

arrived at the inn shortly thereafter and explained about the geological survey.[8]

Unlike his relationship with other acquaintances, Percival was well matched with Shepard, who helped smooth his rough edges and acted as a go-between for him. As they traveled, Percival confided in Shepard about his occasional bouts of melancholy and suicidal thoughts. Yet there were balancing aspects in Percival's personality that touched Shepard, including a strong sense of patriotism, such as his regard for the Revolutionary War hero Israel Putnam. When they visited Wolf Den in Pomfret, the place where Putnam was said to have killed a large wolf preying on livestock in the area, Percival was so moved that he carved his initials on a rock at the entrance of the cave. Shepard recalled, "It was the only place during the tour where he left a similar memorial."[9]

PLATE 1. Nelson Augustus Moore, *Early Autumn Hunt*, 1885. Oil on canvas, 18 × 24 inches. Collection of Marenda and Todd Stitzer. By the nineteenth century, most of the forests in Connecticut had been cut down for farmland, revealing the topography and making it easier for Percival to walk across the state. In this painting, the traprock ridges rise in the background.

PLATE 2. Now called the Metacomet Range, in Percival's time these ridges were known simply as the great wall. Some of the prominent peaks had names such as the Hanging Hills and Mt. Lamentation. This view looking west from South Mountain shows Castle Craig, which opened in 1900, jutting from East Peak. Photograph by Robert Pagini.

PLATE 3. Rising dramatically behind New Haven, West Rock presented a challenge to early geologists, including Percival, because it differed from the main line of traprock running from Massachusetts to Long Island Sound, indicating that the magma had cooled slowly underground instead of on the surface. Photograph by Robert Pagini.

PLATE 4. South Mountain is surrounded by morning mist rising from Merimere Reservoir in Merimere Notch, which was clearly visible from Percival's home in Kensington. In the foreground can be seen the columnar form of traprock. Photograph by Robert Pagini.

PLATE 5. Nelson Augustus Moore, *The Old Percival Place*, 1865. Oil on canvas, 11½ × 16½ inches. Collection of Roy Wiseman and Lisa Kugelman. Percival lived in the red house at the top of the hill near the Congregational Church. Down the hill was the saltbox (just visible near the center of the painting) that had belonged to his grandfather and in which Nelson Augustus Moore was born in 1824.

PLATE 6. Nelson Augustus Moore, *Brook in the Glen*, ca. 1860s. Oil on canvas, 9 × 12 inches. Collection of Derik Pulito. Percival played in this brook as a boy, building palaces out of stones from its banks. He wrote in a poem, "I leave the world of noise and show to wander by my native brook, I ask in Life's unruffled flow no treasure but my friend and book."

PLATE 7. Nelson Augustus Moore, *Saltbox in Winter*, ca. 1880. Oil on canvas, 12 × 18½ inches. Collection of Derik Pulito. Moore's early childhood was spent in the house where Elizabeth Hart, Percival's mother, grew up. In this winter scene, Moore painted sleigh tracks curving down the snowy road past the house.

PLATE 8. Nelson Augustus Moore, *Turkey Hill*, 1899. Oil on canvas, 14⅞ × 24½ inches. Collection of Marenda and Todd Stitzer. Two farmers in Kensington take a break from their labor on a bright summer's day. Moore wrote, "Every sketch or study I have ever made is to me a journal, and every piece I take up brings vividly back to my mind the scene and incidents connected with it."

PLATE 9. Samuel F. B. Morse, *Portrait of Prof. Benjamin Silliman*, 1825. Oil on canvas, 55¼ × 44¼ inches. Yale University Art Gallery. Gift of Bartlett Arkell, B.A. 1886, M.A. 1898, to Silliman College. Benjamin Silliman, Yale professor of chemistry and natural history, stands before a curtain that is pulled back to show West Rock in New Haven. Both Silliman and Percival, his student, were intrigued by what the traprock might reveal about the watery or fiery origins of the earth.

PLATE 10. Nelson Augustus Moore, *A Country Romance*, 1865. Oil on canvas, 22 × 34 inches. Collection of Marenda and Todd Stitzer. Though the hard traprock dominates in the background, there is a soft quality in the foreground where a kneeling man gives flowers to a woman. A similar sentimentality imbues some of Percival's verse, wherein love is linked to flowers.

PLATE 11. Nelson Augustus Moore, *Meriden Notch*, 1893. Oil on canvas, 8½ × 10½ inches. Collection of Derik Pulito. Moore painted this sketch looking toward the south from a point near Percival's home. Percival wrote in a poem about "the gray rocks, and the mountains wrapped in blue, towering far distant through the silent air."

PLATE 12. Nelson Augustus Moore, *The Hanging Hills of Meriden*, 1866. Oil on canvas, 20 × 30 inches. Collection of Marenda and Todd Stitzer. Moore captured the soft light of evening reflected on the water. Of such a sunset he wrote, "The light and shadows were in great masses . . . The middle distance was all in shadows and gray, which brought out the foreground as the light played among the trees beautifully."

PLATE 13. Nelson Augustus Moore, *Summer Calm*, 1867. Oil on canvas, 18 × 28 inches. Collection of Marenda and Todd Stitzer. The subtitle to this painting is *Moore's Upper Pond*, which is fed by water from the traprock ridges to the west. Pondering reflection in nature, Percival wrote that the crystal arch of the sky's "tranquil light takes every hue of mellowness below."

PLATE 14. Nelson Augustus Moore, *Skating on the Upper Pond, Kensington*, 1866. Oil on canvas, 14 × 24 inches. Collection of Todd and Marenda Stitzer. In the winter of 1855, Percival returned briefly to Connecticut to move his belongings into a new home. In his last book he included "Lays of the Season, Winter," which Moore's painting evokes: "Below me rings the lake, / The stars above me burn, / Away the skaters break, / And glide and wheel and turn; / Keen blows the cutting north / Against the wind they drive, / And as they hurry forth, / The air is all alive."

PLATE 15. Nelson Augustus Moore, *The Hanging Hills*, *Pearl Knob*, 1870. Oil on canvas, 19 × 11 inches. Collection of Derik Pulito. This painting depicts the Hanging Hills from the Southington side, looking toward the southeast, and shows the columns of traprock skirted by talus slopes with farms extending out from the base. According to Percival, Pearl Knob was the name given to the highest southwest point of the Hanging Hills.

After Shepard finished his fieldwork, which took six months, he met frequently with Percival to compare notes as he prepared his report. Shepard was amazed that Percival could remember in detail every field and ledge they had examined the prior year. When Shepard asked him to what he owed such a prodigious memory, Percival replied that "it was his custom, on going to bed, to call up, in the darkness and stillness, all the incidents of the day's experience, in their proper order, and cause them to move before him like a diorama through a spiritual morning, noon, and evening." Shepard believed that Percival's ability to concentrate without distracting thoughts "was a mental straightforwardness and conscientiousness, as rare, perhaps, as moral rectitude itself."[10] Shepard published *A Report on the Geological Survey of Connecticut* in 1837, giving the legislators exactly what they wanted, which was an optimistic assessment that was not too long (188 pages), although he stated in the preface that he had not had sufficient time to complete as thorough a study as he would have liked.[11]

From then on, Percival traveled alone, at first by horse at the insistence of the governor who hoped it would speed along the work, and then by foot. Even with the horse, Percival rarely rode it, using it instead as a pack animal for his specimens and tools. Percival wrote in his letter to Roger Sherman Baldwin, a state legislator, that he had "adopted the plan of traveling on foot, which I regret I had not adopted at first, not only as reducing my expenses, but from its superior advantages in carrying out the survey." Expense also dictated his choice of clothing: a neat but drab suit worn to the point of being threadbare, a small brown cloak for winter "of very scanty proportions," no boots, no gloves, no umbrella, and a hat of dubious style. Yet according to Shepard, Percival "endured fatigue and privation with remarkable stanchness."[12]

An additional appropriation from the state legislature enabled Percival to explore the state for eight months in 1837, walking from east to west at intervals of four miles. With his survey still unfinished, he requested and received another appropriation, allowing him to prepare an interim report in January 1838. Percival attempted to do some surveying in the winter but had to stop because of deep snow. It was not until the spring of 1838 that he began to resurvey the state, again traveling from east to west on a route between his former sections, reducing the average width of each section to two miles. The result was that in his two trips he traversed an area covering 4,600 square miles. Richard S. Willis, a friend of Percival's, described the plan as being like a Virginia fence except that "whereas a Virginia fence does not return and take the other angle, Percival's plan did," forming an array of X's, starting from the corner of the state and eventually covering the whole. In actuality, the way Percival surveyed the state was even more complex than that. In a letter to Edward Hitchcock dated September 13, 1838, he described his survey of the western part of the state as not only carried out by traveling east to west, but from south to north, beginning at Long Island Sound and crossing into Massachusetts. "I have then crossed the western Primary in Connecticut thirty-four times at average intervals of about two miles, and have made two sections across Massachusetts in the two southern tiers of towns." This was over a two-year period.[13]

In Percival's interim report to the impatient legislature, he wrote, "I have endeavored to be guided by no other authority than nature; not that I in the least disregarded or undervalued the labors of those who had preceded me, but because I was satisfied that my only chance for determining the system was to confine myself solely to the objects under investigation, and to endeavor to trace my way through by the most careful examination and comparison of them. That I have done so, I can say with confidence, though much of the time under circumstances extremely unfavorable and discouraging."[14]

As Percival walked across the hills and valleys, the ridges and plateaus, he not only identified geological features but also sometimes gave them names, such as calling the rugged hills that crossed Bolton the Bolton Range, tracing it from the Massachusetts border south to where it approached the Connecticut River by Middletown. He clambered over stonewalls built by generations of farmers hauling boulders—called by the locals New England potatoes—from their fields and piling them along the boundary lines. He crossed drumlins that were elliptical hills made out of till left behind by retreating glaciers. Acquiescing to the prevailing belief in a great flood in which icebergs floated—but not Noah's universal flood—Percival thought drumlins might have been formed by vortices of floodwater. He also speculated that the long striations he saw in the rock faces trending northwest to southeast were made by "the action of boulders moved along them by diluvial currents." This was the general belief among geologists at that time. In 1825, Peter Dobson of Vernon, Connecticut, had written to Benjamin Silliman about boulders he had unearthed while constructing a cotton mill. "I think we cannot account of these appearances unless we call in the aid of ice along with water and that they [the boulders] have been worn by being suspended and carried in ice, over rocks and earth, under water." His observation was subsequently published in the *American Journal of Science and Arts*, where Percival is certain to have read it. However, it is important to note that neither Dobson nor Percival had any idea of an immense ice sheet—over a mile thick and covering millions of square miles—grinding across rock. The seminal *Studies on Glaciers* by the Swiss geologist Louis Agassiz would not be published until 1840. Building on the work of other scientists, Agassiz showed the effects of glaciers moving across land during a period of extreme cold he called the Ice Age. Instead, Dobson and Percival envisioned floating icebergs on the underside of which boulders were affixed rather like huge barnacles on the hulls of immense ships.[15]

Walking through the rocky terrain of Montville, Percival identified the anomalous range of hills paralleling the coastal slope that descends to Long Island Sound. Predominantly granitic, there were sections, such as Lantern Hill in North Stonington, where quartz glinted so brightly in the sunlight it could be seen by ships on Long Island Sound. As an example of the ponderous amount of detail Percival included in the report, the following single sentence of ninety-one words on the rocks near Lantern Hill will suffice: "Farther South, in the valley of the Mystic, at Indian Pond Factory, and on the West side of the valley, in a line nearly in the direction of the Quartz vein of Lantern Hill, the granitic gneiss of

FIG. 6.4. John Warner Barber, *Putnam's Wolf Den, Pomfret*. Engraving with ink wash, published in *Connecticut Historical Collections*, 1836. Percival and Shepard visited Wolf Den, where Israel Putnam had killed a wolf. Percival scratched his own initials into the rock near the opening of the cave in honor of Putnam, who had served gallantly in the Revolutionary War.

the present formation, particularly in the beds of the fine-grained red felspathic variety, breaks often in small jointed fragments, and is filled with small veins and seams of crystalline quartz, occasionally accompanied with pyrites and green talc; apparently indicating that the cause which produced the quartz vein of Lantern Hill was there operative."[16]

Percival was also intrigued by the Pomperaug Valley in the southwest corner of the state because it was like a smaller version of the Connecticut Valley, with the valley floor underlain by sedimentary rock and walled by metamorphic rock. Running through it were traprock ridges that Percival mapped with remarkable accuracy. The width of his lines meticulously drawn in black ink indicated the size, location, and curve of the rock.

In the northwest corner of the state, Percival found hills and plateaus approximately one thousand feet higher than those in the eastern uplands. Part of the Berkshire Range that is the southern extension of the Green Mountains, this area is the eroded remnant of the ancient Appalachian Mountains. However, determining the age and origin of the uplands was not as much of a concern to Percival as was the potential for ore because it was in this corner of the state that the economically important iron quarries were located, one of the largest being near Ore Hill in Litchfield County. For the same reason, he was also interested in the marble valleys, through which the Housatonic River flowed.

Unfortunately for modern amateur geologists, Percival had to locate rock by existing topographic and cultural features, such as brooks, roads, bridges, farms, or historic places, such as Putnam's Wolf Den. For example, in attempting to pinpoint for readers of the report the location of a line of "very fine-grained, light bluish grey ferruginous" or iron-containing rocks, Percival wrote that the line "crosses the Humphreysville Turnpike near the Gate S. E. of that village, and is observed in various points S. W. of Bethany, particularly West of the North branch of Bladen's Brook." In trying to pinpoint another rock formation, he wrote that it extended "to the Housatonic, near Zoar Bridge, where it crosses that river in quite a narrow range, and is continued up the valley of Eight Mile river, at least to Quaker's Farms (Oxford)." None of this is very helpful today since the gate on the turnpike is long gone, as is the farm on Eight Mile River. However, what Percival could not do by words he could do visually by means of the map that he drew to accompany the report.[17]

In all the places that he visited, Percival chipped out specimens. Then each evening he labeled each specimen including the precise location and the relationship between the specimens. As he wrote in his letter to Baldwin, "While traveling, it was my practice to rise early, in the longer days generally at dawn; in the shorter generally I got breakfast and was on my way by daybreak. I continued, scarcely with any relaxation, as long as I had daylight, and then was generally obliged to sit up till midnight, not unfrequently till one o'clock, a.m., in order to complete my notes and arrange my specimens. This was continued, not only week after week, but month after month, almost without cessation."[18]

Using the only classification scheme available at the time for categorizing the geologic age of the various formations he encountered, Percival divided the rocks into three classes: primary (igneous), secondary (sedimentary), and trap (by which Percival meant volcanic in origin). Found in the uplands, the rock labeled as primary came first and was therefore older, or as Percival called it, "original material." Secondary rock, found mainly in the valleys, often contained fragments of primary rock due to erosion, indicating it was formed later. The secondary rock was principally sandstone and shale. In studying the primary rock, Percival realized that the eastern and western uplands differed, one indication being "an apparent change in the axes of the crystals."[19] To Percival, there was a "distinct frontier" between the metamorphic and igneous rocks forming the uplands bordering the eastern side of the Connecticut Valley and the sedimentary rocks and traprock of the valley itself. Perplexed, he wrote in the report, "It is true, there are formations in the two different sections [eastern and western uplands], which present some striking resemblances to each other; but they are entirely detached, not merely by the interposition of the Secondary, but by that of other Primary formations." It is now known that the reason for this detachment has to do with plate tectonics, with the eastern and western uplands being separate blocks of crust (known as terranes) bounded by faults. The Connecticut Valley is a failed rift valley that is part of a different block known as the Newark terrane. While there was no way for Percival to solve this conundrum with a hammer and chisel for tools (the solution had to await the development of technology, including sonar to explore the Atlantic seafloor), it is to his great credit that he made the observation. It is also to his credit that he avoided putting his ideas about the transition between the older Paleozoic and younger Mesozoic rocks (terms that were not in use) into the report, writing that "the system is very complex, and to do justice to its development requires ample time and reasonable resources." For the purposes of the survey, he considered himself merely an observer reporting on what he had seen.[20]

The traprock presented another major challenge. Percival recognized that although most of the traprock in Connecticut was extrusive, at certain locations it was intrusive, including East Rock, West Rock, and Sleeping Giant (also known as Mount Carmel). Both varieties were formed by melted rock, or magma, deep within the earth that either cooled beneath the surface to form intrusive diabase or dolerite, or emerged from fissures as lava to form extrusive basalt. Percival used the phrase "volcanic action" for lava that overflowed the land to differentiate it from an explosive eruption from a volcano such as Mount Vesuvius. However, there was great variation, for example, if "the volcanic action" took place under water, the lava took on a rounded form that appropriately came to be known as pillow basalt. What Percival concluded was that there was not one long continuous fissure that allowed magma to upwell through the sedimentary strata, but instead a series of roughly parallel fissures through which magma rose at different times in "a certain systemic order." The existence of separate flows helped explain the differences in the traprock. Although Percival did not name the lava flows, they are now called, from the oldest to the youngest in succession, the Talcott Basalt, the Holyoke Basalt, and the Hampden Basalt. Sedimentation, erosion, faulting, and tilting of the strata had over an enormous period of time exposed the traprock. As had Hutton before him, Percival realized these processes were ongoing.[21]

The igneous origin of traprock also meant there were no fossils in it as there were in sedimentary rock, such as sandstone and shale. On this point Percival was emphatic, as he made clear in a letter to Hitchcock. Because Hitchcock believed in Noah's flood, he had asked Percival to be on the lookout for fossils. Percival replied:

> I endeavor to be guided in my scientific pursuits by a maxim of Humboldt's in his Personal Narrative: "Our business as men of science is not with the origin of things but with their present state." Science can determine how things *are*. Speculation may guess how they *were*. In conformity with this principle I replied to Governor Edwards, who observed that he thought the business of geology was to determine how the earth *was* made, "No, sir, it is the business of geogony, if such a science were possible, to de-

termine how the earth *was* made. It is the business of geology to determine how the earth *is* made, or at least that
part of it within the limits of our observation." With these
views I must decline answering your queries. I have indulged in some speculations as to the origin of rocks, but
I endeavor to keep my speculations entirely distinct from
my observations and generalizations, or rather my observations of the particular and the general. My great aim has
been to determine precisely the different kinds of Primary
rocks and their system of arrangement, persuaded that until that is done speculations as to origins must be but poor
guess work. It does appear to me that geology is too much
geogony for the true interests of science.[22]

By 1840, Percival had completed eleven manuscript volumes,
amounting to 1,500 pages written in miniscule handwriting with
many abbreviations. He had collected eight thousand specimens:
"each specimen intended to illustrate something peculiar and no-
ticed in my notes—all my specimens marked on the papers en-
closing them, and checked in my note-books so that I knew their
precise locality and could again trace them to the spot where I
found them." It took Percival seven years because he was not satisfied with his data, considering it incomplete; his obsessive perfectionism and his frustration at the magnitude of unanswered
questions posed by the data were to blame. When he requested yet
more funding in 1841, the new governor, William Ellsworth, and
the legislators refused, forcing him to publish the *Report on the
Geology of the State of Connecticut* in 1842. He considered it "a hasty
outline . . . under circumstances little calculated for cool consid-
eration." His hasty outline was 495 pages long. It also included a
map of unsurpassed exactitude. Jelle Zeilinga de Boer wrote of
Percival in *Stories in Stone: How Geology Influenced Connecticut History*, "On his map, he delineates most major rock types with an accuracy that leaves even contemporary geologists speechless. These
days, geologists might spend several years mapping a single quad-
rangle. Percival surveyed all ninety-nine in just seven years."[23]

Shepard was impressed by Percival's desire to discover the general laws of nature, noting that his interests were much broader than geology. "While he could sympathize perfectly, he said, with those who threw their whole force into a single study, he felt himself attracted equally by the entire circle of nature, and thought omniscience a nobler object of ambition than any one science," Shepard explained. "He admitted that the search after all knowledge is incompatible with eminence in any particular department; but he believed that it affords higher pleasure to the mind, and confers ability to do significant service to mankind in pointing out the grand connections, the general laws, of nature."[24]

The *American Journal of Science and Arts* reviewed the report in the January 1843 issue, heaping praise on it, although the reviewer noted it would probably only be read by geologists, certainly not the legislators who had voted for its funding. However, when coupled with the report by Shepard, it had the desired effect on the economy by promoting mining and quarrying. Five years after it was published, the Beckley blast furnace was built in East Canaan, producing iron for the wheels of railroad cars. Another new industry in the Connecticut Valley was the quarrying and crushing of traprock for railroad embankments. Percival and Shepard had not found gold, thus precluding a gold rush in Connecticut similar to that set in motion by the 1848 discoveries at Sutter's Creek in California; nor had they found deposits of hard coal needed for the blast furnaces as had been found in abundance in Pennsylvania. However, they did point out the existence of many minerals of a more humdrum nature, such as feldspar and mica, which were nonetheless important industrial commodities. It was just this type of information that the geological survey was meant to reveal.

The question remained whether Percival's work contributed to the advancement of geology. James D. Dana (who was Silliman's successor as professor of natural history and geology at Yale as well as his son-in-law) considered Percival's work on fissures to be foundational to his own research on how mountain ranges were built. In a paper published in 1848, Dana wrote, "Before proceeding farther, it is important to understand the general character of fissures; and we present a case to the point from the map accompanying the elaborate report of Dr. J. G. Percival on the Geology of Connecticut—a work of vast labor, and of minute and cautious research by one of the ablest men in America. Dr. Percival has afforded us a key to this subject of the highest value, by the results of his investigations among the trap dikes of New England."[25] After Percival's death, Dana wrote a letter to Julius Ward in which he summed up his respect for Percival: "In the expression Percival the geologist, few will recognize a reference to Percival the poet, and yet in my opinion, no one in the country has done better work in geology or work of greater value to science."

Geology has changed enormously since then and even Dana's theories on mountain ranges were long ago relegated to the dustbins of science. Regardless, Percival's work mattered at a time when geology was gaining an identity independent of traditional chemistry and physics. In a letter to a state legislator, Percival stressed that geology was a scientific undertaking and geologists were professionals who could serve as intelligent guides in the search for ores and minerals, thereby increasing the odds of success. Geology had come a long way since Silliman's early days at Yale, when his laboratory was down in the dark cellar. Percival had done his part in bringing geology up into the light, proving that it was both scientifically important and economically essential.[26]

SEVEN

An Intermezzo of Music and Language

Whenever winter storms forced Percival to take a break from traversing Connecticut, he would retreat to his apartment in New Haven. He lived on the third floor of an empty building that had once been a state hospital. The place was cluttered and knee-deep in dust. He slept on a dirty cot covered by two even dirtier blankets and secured the front door with a piece of rope. None of this mattered to Percival. What mattered was that he had three large rooms: in the first room were his living quarters; in the second was his enormous rock collection (threatening the weight-bearing capacity of the floor); and in the third was his library of approximately ten thousand books. Maps and papers were pinned to the walls. After the geological report was published, it was just the place for a quasi-recluse to continue his linguistic studies with the same singularity of purpose and concentration he had brought to poetry and geology. If visitors came, he spoke with them in the hallway but did not invite them into the apartment. Even when Henry Wadsworth Longfellow came to call, Percival met him in the hospital's reception room on the first floor.[1]

Percival studied at least twenty-four languages, among them Gaelic, Czech, Wallachian, Sanskrit, Bengalese, and Eskimo. He also visited Indian tribes living near Long Island Sound to learn their language. He was a proficient translator from the ancient languages of Hebrew, Greek, and Latin as well as from the modern languages of French, Italian, and German. In his essay "James

Gates Percival, Student of German Culture," Adolph B. Benson wrote, "He seems to have been able to read every European language except Turkish, including ancient and modern forms, and to have had a good knowledge of some Oriental dialects. Language to him was the first key to history and philosophy, the *open-sesame* to the thoughts of nations and individuals. So Percival became one of the first real philologists of the United States."[2]

Percival had a special interest in German, having taught himself the language in 1823, writing to a friend, "I have been dipping into [German], and a *strange* language it is in sound and construction—sucking in its gutturals like a whirlpool, *augh*—hissing out its sibilants like a goose, *eech*—and rolling round its oblique diphthongs like a sailor his quid, *foieer.*"[3] His interest was driven in part by his desire to read the books being published by German scholars in the new fields of comparative philology and etymology, as well as in geology. Percival advanced so rapidly in his studies that before long he was reading the works of Goethe and Schiller, bringing them to the attention of American readers by publishing his translations in New Haven newspapers and magazines. He also gave public readings and lectures mainly attended by members of the Yale community who were impressed by his mastery of German even though, according to Julius Ward, Percival "had no acquaintance with the niceties of pronunciation."[4]

In an essay published in the *New Haven Daily Palladium,* in which he analyzed excerpts from Goethe and Schiller, Percival wrote, "Where the character is subjective, habitually fixed in the feeling of self-emotions, there Schiller is the favored author; where it is objective, living not within self-consciousness, but externalized, if I may use such a word, in the observation of the world without, there Goethe is preferred. Goethe, in one word, wins and fascinates; Schiller compels and subdues. Goethe is idolized by the Germans; Schiller is worshipped." At the end of the essay he admitted that translating poetry was more difficult than composing original poetry, writing, "I can only regret that I have not been able to do better justice to [Goethe and Schiller] in my translation." He worried that his translations showed "an educational and scholastic knowledge" of the language but not "an intimate knowledge," so whenever possible he corresponded with other scholars, including George Ticknor, a respected professor of languages at Harvard.[5]

As Benson pointed out, Percival was not merely interested in mastering a language or translating verse; he was interested in the nature of language itself, how it developed over time and how it influenced culture. Seeking answers, he acquired the seminal works by the German linguists Franz Bopp and Jacob Grimm, who was best known for his collection of folklore collected with his brother Wilhelm. He placed large orders at Howe's Bookstore for books in Slavic. As in geology, Percival felt a compulsion to find an overarching system uniting all languages. This led him to study ancient languages that were still spoken in Europe, such as Basque, considered to be one of the oldest languages on earth. Lucius W. Fitch wrote in a biographical sketch of Percival that "linguistic science became to him a key to infinitely more than a dry and barren knowledge of words; it not only classified the wondrously varied tribes of men according to their mutual relations of descent and consanguinity, but it became the foundation of the philosophy which unlocked for him, as a student of mankind, the inmost recesses of the heart."[6]

Benson considered Percival's study of German to be the opening of a door to other languages, introducing him to "the wealth of the Russian folk-songs, though Percival in the course of time learned to read all the important Slavonic dialects."[7] In this regard, Percival began to correspond in 1835 with Talvj, who combined the initials of her full name—Therese Albertine Louise von Jakob—into her exotic pseudonym. Beautiful, brilliant, and German, Talvj was the daughter of a professor who moved his family frequently during her childhood: from Halle in Prussian Saxony to Kharkov and then to St. Petersburg before returning to Halle after the Napoleonic Wars. Along the way, Talvj learned Ukrainian, Russian, and Serbian and collected folksongs and poems. After the family's return to Halle, Talvj met and married Edward Robinson, an American minister who was studying in Prussia. Coincidentally, Robinson was from Southington, on the western side of the traprock near Kensington. He and Percival had studied together as young teenagers preparing for entry to Yale.

FIG. 7.1. Unidentified artist, *Portrait of Talvj*. Etching published in *The Life and Works of Therese Robinson*, by Irma Elizabeth Voigt, 1913. The linguist Therese Robinson, known as Talvj, corresponded with Percival, hoping that he would collaborate with her on German and Slavic translations. Percival was fluent in German and had translated some of Goethe's works.

After the Robinsons came to the United States, Talvj returned to her work, attempting to versify Russian poetry for a book on the literature of the Slavic nations, but she needed help. For his part, Percival owned two of Talvj's books on Serbian folksongs that had been praised by Goethe, and he had some questions about her translation. Talvj and Percival may have heard about each other through Professor Ticknor or Dr. George Hayward, who were mutual acquaintances, or through Talvj's husband. No matter how the introduction came about, it seems that Percival initiated the correspondence with Talvj, but he was so shy toward women he sent the letter to her husband. Talvj responded forthrightly, "Since the first part of your letter concerns me, although it is addressed to my husband, I will answer it myself." In his reply, this time written directly to her, Percival expressed his desire to collaborate, but he warned her that his time of late had been occupied with other pursuits and that she had better "prepare yourself for the contingency of a disappointment." Then he explained his approach to translation, attempting to ascertain whether they were in agreement: "I had rather that [translation] be strictly faithful, though a little inferior in composition, than that it be perfect as a composition, yet unfaithful to the original. I have applied these principles in several translations that I have published in one of the New Haven newspapers, copies of which I sent to Professor Ticknor and Dr. George Hayward."

Unfortunately, although Percival truly wanted to work with Talvj, he was already committed to the Connecticut geological report and was in the process of surveying the state with Charles Shepard. He asked whether she could wait awhile, to which she agreed, but then he continued to put her off. His geological work was demanding all his time. Talvj became disheartened. Eventually, she included in an article for *North American Review* (July 1836) some Russian folksongs Percival had translated, but that was the extent of their partnership.[8] In his essay "Talvj's Correspondence with James Gates Percival," Arthur P. Coleman wrote of her disappointment, "She hoped, when she discovered Percival, who also would have liked to perform this service, that she had found the one who could make her dream a reality. But Percival was a poor reed to lean upon, as everyone found who tried to work with him, and she was doomed to disappointment and disillusion."[9]

Despite his inability to work with Talvj, Percival continued his study of language even while he was conducting the geological survey, often entertaining Shepard with impromptu lectures on the subject. Shepard recalled:

> Percival's favorite topics, when evening came and we rested from our stony labors, were the modern languages and the philosophy of universal grammar. They seemed to have filled the niches in his heart from which he had banished, or tried to banish, the Muses. The subtle refinements of Bopp were a perpetual luxury to him; he derived language from language as easily as word from word; and once started in the intricacies of the Russian or the Basque, there was no predicting the end of the discourse. Thus were thrown away, upon a solitary listener, midnight lectures which would have done honor to the classrooms of Berlin or the Sorbonne.[10]

Benson concurred with Shepard's assessment, writing emphatically about Percival's astonishing linguistic abilities: "Percival was beyond doubt one of the foremost of his time in this land; indeed, he surpassed in most respects the ability of his contemporaries, and in comparative, scientific study anticipated the better-known scholars of language chronologically by several years."[11]

Percival's friends considered him a language wizard. Dr. Hayward claimed he was nearly the equal of Cardinal Guiseppe Mezzofanti (1774–1849), who was said to be fluent in thirty-eight languages with some knowledge of an additional eighty-eight. William G. Webster, the son of Noah Webster, recalled an example of Percival's wizardry that took place during the presidential campaign of William Henry Harrison: "During the Harrison campaign we belonged to a club of patriotic Whigs, whose weekly meetings were held at my house to compose and sing the songs of this exciting period. Richard S. Willis was our conductor, and Percival our poet. Willis would select some national German melody or chorus, and we would call on Percival for the words to be adapted to the air. Retiring to my library, he would in an incredibly short time, return with some patriotic, spirit-stirring stanzas, that afterwards lent so much enthusiasm to that exciting period."[12]

One of Percival's celebratory songs that had nothing to do with German was titled "Success to Tippecanoe." Tippecanoe was Harrison's nickname and was a reference to the battle of Tippecanoe he had fought against the Shawnee leader Tecumseh. Enamored of Harrison, Percival had added a rousing chorus of "Old Tip is a coming from Ohi O! Old Tip is a coming from Ohi O!" When Harrison fell seriously ill and died on April 4, 1841, only thirty-one days after taking office, Percival, in his grief, wrote three of the four hymns sung in commemoration at the Center Church in New Haven.[13]

Occasionally, Percival would visit William Webster in his home, sit down at the piano and pick out single notes in an effort to write music, but more times than not, he unknowingly repeated tunes he had learned as a child. He acquired an accordion and also attempted to learn how to play flute and guitar. Richard Willis, then a student at Yale, wrote that Percival tried to develop a new theory of music and would show up at Willis's room at all hours of the day and night seeking assistance. "No master of the art of writing music, he ordinarily brought his compositions jotted down in illegible hieroglyphics of his own, and wished to have them reduced to shape." To Willis, when Percival was making music, he had "the appearance of a minstrel come down from another age."[14]

As the recollections of Webster and Willis make clear, during this period Percival had begun to mellow, and the melancholy, which in the past had been like a millstone, had lifted a little. Never a misanthrope despite his monkish behavior, he developed a close circle of friends, dubbed the Percival Club, who met for dinner and conversation, sometimes extending far into the night. He followed politics closely, attended a Whig convention in the state, and wrote numerous letters to newspapers, periodicals, and politicians. Percival even wrote songs, often in German, for The Sing-Song Club in New Haven and occasionally tried to solo, accompanying himself on his accordion, but his voice was so soft that no one could hear him. He also attended concerts, and when a famous Norwegian violinist performed in New Haven, Percival presented him with a celebratory poem he had written in Danish.

However, his old problems with perfectionism had not gone away. When Webster hired him to work on the second edition of his father's dictionary, Percival never got past the letter B. "I have known him to spend two or three days on the investigation of a single word," Webster remarked, "and had the character of our work been such as to justify the delay consequent on such minute investigation, his labors would have been invaluable."[15]

Still a solitary wanderer, Percival disappeared for weeks at a time without telling his friends where he was going, sometimes returning in the middle of the night. Often these trips were to neighboring states for geological purposes, such as to survey mines. Also during this period he occasionally got into squabbles with other geologists when they did not give him enough credit for his ideas on the formation of traprock, writing to Lyell somewhat petulantly, "I cannot but feel a wish to receive the credit (whatever it may be) justly due me for a system which I have worked out with so much time & labor." He continued to run up a hefty tab ordering books at Howe's Bookstore that left him on the verge of destitution. However, these problems did not hobble him as much as they once had, nor were they a barrier to forming friendships.[16]

In 1843, Percival published *The Dream of a Day*, a collection of poems written over a sixteen-year period beginning in 1827, the year *Clio III* was published. The poems were presented basically in chronological order except for the first one, from which the title of the book was taken. In line with his language studies, there were many translations from Russian, German, Norwegian, and other languages. There was also a section dedicated to unusual poetic forms, going far beyond basic iambic to arcane "choriambic polyschematist." Percival's goal was to open his readers to an international world of verse, which was the same goal Talvj set for her books. He was also a little apologetic, writing in the preface:

> In the long interval which has elapsed since the publication of my last volume of poems (sixteen years) I have been most of the time engaged in pursuits which have little or no relation to poetical studies, or which have been peculiarly adverse to them; consequently, during this period, the composition of verse has been to me only an occasional amusement or exercise. As such, I offer this volume; not as the fruits of a continued and regular study of an art, which, for the high principles it involves, and the great powers which it demands for its true and most successful cultivation, deserves to hold a place in the first rank.[17]

The title poem of *The Dream of a Day* is about finding renewed inspiration, rising again into the empyrean heights of creative ecstasy. In his earlier poems, in which he envisioned a sublime world, the spirits that appeared to him were sometimes antagonistic and intimidating, but since then the spirits had become benign. In the poem, Percival perceived himself as dreaming awake when suddenly, "A spirit stood before me half unseen, / Majestic and severe, yet o'er him played a genial light." The spirit tells Percival to hold on and to continue even though there have been long years of bitter toil. It is for Percival to "behold the true, to feel the pure, to know the good and lovely," all of which endure, and it is his mission to "reveal the secrets nature has unveiled" to him.

The Dream of a Day received a few positive reviews. An enthusiastic reviewer in the *New York Evangelist* had only one criticism, which concerned Percival's "apparent want of interest in the pre-vailing religion of his country. We say apparent, for we cannot think him really indifferent." *The Knickerbocker* also recommended the book, noting that Percival was a frequent contributor. A decid-edly lukewarm review, unsigned but most likely written by Ralph Waldo Emerson, was published in *The Dial* in July 1843. Emerson, who was seven years younger than Percival, was familiar with his poetry, grouping him rather disdainfully with Richard Henry Dana Sr. and William Cullen Bryant. While praising him for the thorough workmanship of his translations and his exploration of ancient poetic measures, Emerson stated, "unhappily this dil-igence is not without its dangers" because the focus on poetry as an art form drained it of its emotional power. "Our bard has not quite so much fire as we had looked for, grows warm but does not ignite; those sixteen years of 'adverse' studies have had their effect on Pegasus, who now trots soundly and resolutely on, but forbears rash motions, and never runs away from us."[18]

The Dream of a Day was Percival's last published book, but de-spite what had been said in the review, Pegasus had not forgotten he had wings. And though it is only conjecture, those wings may have carried him briefly into the world of Thoreau, with whom he shared the close personal friendship of the Hayward family of Boston—Percival with Dr. George Hayward, and Thoreau with his son, Charles Hayward, who died of typhoid at the age of twen-ty-one.[19] In 1842, a year before the review appeared in *The Dial*, Emerson was serving as temporary editor of the struggling pub-lication, trying to find content to fill up the July issue. He asked Thoreau, about to turn twenty-five years old, to be his assistant and to write a piece on the natural history component of Edward Hitchcock's Massachusetts survey. *The Natural History of Massa-chusetts* was basically an inventory, as the title page made clear: "On the Fishes, Reptiles, and Birds; Herbaceous Plants and Quad-rupeds; the Insects Injurious to Vegetation; and Invertebrate An-imals of Massachusetts." Finding it to be dry reading, Thoreau turned to his own knowledge and experience to breathe some life into the creatures mentioned. Emerson did not think much of Tho-reau's essay, but he printed it in *The Dial* anyway, thereby providing readers their first glimpse of Thoreau's ability in prose while also bringing attention to Hitchcock's two reports.

Like Percival, Thoreau was already an inveterate walker who was more alive when he was outside than in. He loved the classics and had translated *Prometheus Bound* just as Percival had done when he was the same age. From Emerson's library, Thoreau borrowed books on Sanskrit and Hindu holy texts written by William Jones, books that Percival also owned and had used in his philological studies. He devoured Lyell's *Principles of Geology*, finding Lyell to be an exhilarating guide to the beginnings of an ancient and infinite earth. He tried to understand how science could be brought into balance with all the other aspects of his life, writing at the end of *The Dial* essay, "Wisdom does not inspect, but beholds. We must look a long time before we see."

Three years later, in 1845, Thoreau built his house on Walden Pond and there one winter night he had an unusual visitor from Connecticut, whom Thoreau described as all brain, who could discourse brilliantly about everything without stopping, until Thoreau joyously concluded that the seams of his house were in danger of bursting open from sheer intellectual atmospheric pressure:

> I should not forget that during my last winter at the pond there was another welcome visitor, who at one time came through the village, through the snow and rain and darkness, till he saw my lamp through the trees, and shared with me some long winter evenings. One of the last of the philosophers—Connecticut gave him to the world—he peddled first her wares, afterwards, as he declares, his brains. These he peddles still, prompting God and disgracing man, bearing for fruit his brain only, like the nut its kernel.

The two men talked and talked, and when day came, they left the house and "sauntered" through the woods—still talking.

> We waded so gently and reverently, or we pulled together so smoothly, that the fishes of thought were not scared from the stream, nor feared any angle on the bank, but came and went grandly, like the clouds which float through the west-

ern sky, and the mother-o'-pearl flocks which sometimes form and dissolve there. There we worked revising mythology, rounding a fable here and there, and building castles in the air for which earth offered no worthy founder.

Thoreau did not provide the visitor's name. On the basis of text comparison between the Walden passage and a journal entry dated May 9, 1853, scholars have understandably assumed it was his friend Bronson Alcott, who also hailed from Connecticut. However, Alcott helped build the house and often visited on Sunday afternoons. His ideas and demeanor were well known to Thoreau, who described him in the entry as "broad, genial, but indefinite; some would say feeble; forever feeling about vainly in his speech and touching nothing. But this is a very negative account of him, for he thus suggests far more than the sharp and definite practical mind."

The stranger who showed up one winter's night, forcing open the seams of the house with the power of his discourse, does not sound like Alcott. He sounds for all the world like Percival.[20]

EIGHT

West to the Frontier of Wisconsin

Percival's growing reputation as a geologist opened up employment opportunities that drew him away from his solitary studies. Close to home, he was hired to complete a survey for a railroad line that would run from New Haven to Fishkill, New York. Benjamin Noyes, a New Haven businessman, wrote, "He performed the work, aided by an assistant, and made a line report, designating the entire route by roads, houses, streams, etc. so that to this day there has never been any difficulty in recognizing his survey mile by mile; and it has been a constant reference in subsequent surveys."[1] As word spread that hiring Percival was a smart business decision despite his strange behavior, he began to travel far beyond the borders of Connecticut, going north to assess coal and iron mines in Nova Scotia and New Brunswick, Canada; west to assess rocky islands in Lake Erie, among them the Bass Islands and Edwards Island (now Gibraltar Island); and then southwest through Missouri and the Ozarks to survey for lead.[2]

A soft, grey metal easily extracted from ore, lead had been used extensively for pipes in the Roman Empire. In fact, the Latin root of the word plumbing is *plumbum*, meaning lead. Over the centuries it had been used in numerous products, such as utensils made of pewter (an alloy of tin and lead), bullets, paint, and glass. However, in the nineteenth century, the demand for lead had begun to rise (and was about to soar) as major cities began to build municipal water systems.

Percival's most significant commission came in 1853 when F. E. Phelps, president of the American Mining Company, hired him to determine the size and depth of lead deposits in Illinois and Wisconsin.[3] The first deposits had been found in the southwestern corner of Wisconsin in 1826, causing a surge of prospectors and speculators into the area, which was not yet a U.S. territory. Within three years, more than four thousand miners had arrived. Finding accommodations nonexistent, they took on the moniker "badgers" because they lived in caves just as badgers lived in holes—a moniker that would eventually be used for the entire state. New settlements had sprung up with names such as Mineral Point, New Diggings, Black Jack, and Hard Scrabble—appropriate names given that mining was a rugged and dangerous profession, making a few people very rich and many people very poor.

Because the American Mining Company had operations in the vicinity, Percival went to the little town of Hazel Green, which had recently changed its name from Hard Scrabble in a bid to improve its image. Hazel Green had a population of approximately six hundred, with eight stores, four churches, one school, and four hotels. Indicative of a grandeur more hoped for than real, one of the hotels was named The Wisconsin House and another was named The Empire House. The idea of Hazel Green's being part of an empire was not as far-fetched as it may seem, aligning as it did with the term "Manifest Destiny" that had first been used in the mid-1840s by John O'Sullivan in *The Democratic Review*. It meant that only westward expansion would fulfill America's divine right "to overspread the continent allotted by Providence for the free development of our yearly multiplying millions," as O'Sullivan grandly put it. Even Thoreau felt the pull westward on his walks in Concord, considering it "the prevailing tendency of my countrymen. I must walk toward Oregon, and not Europe." Thoreau would have disagreed with O'Sullivan that the west was the nation's God-given right, but he would have agreed that the east was set in its ways, while the west represented "the spirit of enterprise and adventure."[4] Perhaps Percival felt that pull as well. At the very least, he found Hazel Green to be rich with geological potential and its cit-

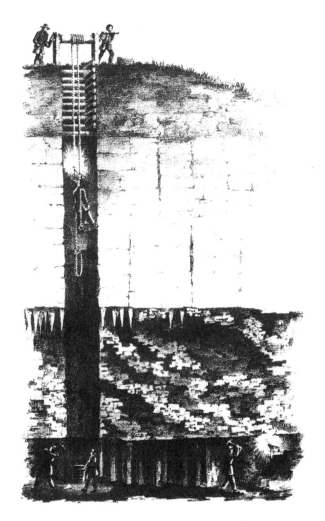

FIG. 8.1. Unidentified artist, *Lead Mine*. Etching published in 1932 in *The Wisconsin Lead Region* by Joseph Schafer, State Historical Society of Wisconsin. This cross-section of a lead mine was originally in a report by the geologist David Dale Owen. Two men work a windlass to lower a miner down a shaft to where other miners remove ore with pickaxes. The miner wears a headlamp and stands on an ore bucket.

izens enthralled with the prospects of empire-like wealth obtain-
able merely by digging in the ground.

As Americans pushed westward into unexplored country, there
was a get-rich-quick approach to mining and quarrying that ultimately degraded both men and land. Using pickaxes, chisels, crow-
bars, shovels, and blasting powder to get out the most accessible
ore found in shallow crevice deposits, the small mining crews usually ignored the ore that was harder to reach and that required
pumping water out of the shafts. They also ignored other minerals, such as zinc, dumping it in the soaring heaps of mine tailings.
The timbering of mines to prevent collapse of shafts was haphaz-
ard at best. To those dangers was added another—lead was toxic
if ingested by miners eating food with lead-coated hands. Furthermore, the smelting of lead put toxic fumes in the air. One of the
signs of lead poisoning was that a miner's gums turned blue due
to anemia, but because the symptoms came on slowly, they were
often ignored. Like the edgy names of the mines, the equally edgy
names of the miners gave evidence of a rough life, such as Patch
Eye John, Bloody Kentuck, and Bullet Neck Green.[5]

By contrast, in Europe, mining was an honorable profession
taught by guilds and at prestigious mining schools, one of the
most famous being the academy at Freiberg in Germany, which
had been under the able direction of Abraham Gottlob Werner.
The only ameliorating factor in Wisconsin was that some of the
new arrivals were immigrant miners from Cornwall in Great Britain who brought with them their knowledge of hard-rock mining
techniques. According to Joseph Schafer in his book *The Wisconsin Lead Region*, the Cornish were known as "Cousin Jacks" and
"ranked as the most skillful practical miners, making good wages
from diggings which Americans were ready to abandon."[6]

In 1847, the local newspaper in Mineral Point reported that the
town's furnaces were producing 43,800 pounds of lead each day.
Unfortunately, that figure represented the peak. The next year productivity began to decline for two reasons: the use of primitive
mining methods that relied on limited surface deposits, and the
California Gold Rush, which attracted miners looking to make an
easy fortune. It is estimated that Mineral Point alone lost at least

seven hundred miners to the gold fields. As one regional historian wrote, "With the announcement of the existence of wealth
across the continent, the bone and sinew of this section lent a
willing ear to the reports, and having realized a confirmation of
what they heard, girded up their portables and joined the army of
miners which crossed the plains, and became pioneers in the new
El Dorado."[7]

Percival found the region beautiful but markedly different from
Connecticut. Instead of clapboard homes there were log cabins; instead of stonewalls there were split rail fences. The prairie was broken by bluffs and mounds about the same height as Connecticut's
traprock ridges, but there the similarity ended, for these were not
basalt but mainly limestone. It was easier to conduct a survey in
Connecticut, where most of the land had been cleared for farm-
ing, than to conduct one in Wisconsin, where the land was either
forest or prairie.

In a letter to Edward C. Herrick, who was a Yale librarian and
a stalwart friend, Percival wrote a few months after his arrival,
"This is truly a rich and beautiful country. Besides its vast mineral resources, it is rich in surface and subsoil, the last peculiar
to the mining region, and beautiful exceedingly, whether broken
woodland or rolling prairie." He then gave Herrick an example of
the colorful mining lingo he often heard from prospectors, which
he found comical in its total lack of geological knowledge: "I was
staked on a prospect, and after prospecting several days I struck
a lead and raised a lot of bully minerals, but it was only a bunch
in a chimney, without any opening; so I petered out, and a sucker
jumped me." Sucker was the term used for a prospector who was
like a green shoot on a bush, appearing in the spring and disap-
pearing in the autumn. To "jump" a claim meant to seize mining
rights "staked" by another prospector.[8]

Despite making fun of prospectors, Percival found the people in
Hazel Green to be congenial. Accustomed to miners of the strangest sort, they accepted him as he was, laughing politely instead of
scoffing at his peculiarities. Indeed, it didn't take long before stories about Percival were common coin in Hazel Green, but they
were not mean-spirited. For example, one of the stories was about

Percival's stay in a hotel filled with boisterous miners not long after his arrival. Their all-hours-of-the-night carousing included stomping up and down the stairs in heavy boots, keeping Percival awake. His revenge was not to pull out a pistol or to resort to a bottle of whiskey but to write "a caustic poem in Greek" in which the noisy boarders "were neatly done up."[9]

It is also true that the social climate in Hazel Green was not as intellectually fraught as in New Haven, where among Percival's friends there was an unspoken competition to see who was the penultimate genius among geniuses, the ultimate genius being Percival himself. As a result, he felt at ease in Hazel Green, and the mellowing of his personality that had begun in New Haven continued apace. One local man wrote, "However eccentric or forbidding Dr. Percival appeared to outside observers, in the private social circle he was full of cheer and mirth, his utterances often sparkling with wit and wisdom." Another man expressed the admiration, verging on awe, the people of Hazel Green felt for Percival: "He impressed you as a man of power. Whatever he said meant something."[10]

Percival immediately set to work traveling with William Warner, the American Mining Company's representative who lived in Hazel Green. The company was considering leasing 1,500 acres, erecting two 250-horse-power engines, and draining the land so that more extensive mining could be carried out. The decision would be made on the basis of Percival's findings. Townspeople and miners were amazed by his capacity for work, which kept him from turning homeward until late each day. One man recalled that "he entered upon his new field of labor in the mines with much zeal and pleasure, which seemed to increase with the prosecution of his researches, whether viewing the rocky bluff or a stream or examining the debris from some mineral range, with the view of deducing some facts connected with industrial science for the benefit of mining."[11]

On September 28, 1853, five months after beginning his work for the American Mining Company, Percival was "suddenly attacked with a chill, on issuing from a mine on a cold raw day." The mine was near Fever River (now known as the Galena River, Galena being the name for lead ore), where there had been much sickness of an unknown kind. In a letter to Herrick written a month later, Percival wrote, "I had been very laboriously and, as I thought, successfully employed; and, at my attack, had increased the number of my entries into mines to one hundred and twenty. On Monday I had been out all day in mines and on surface explorations, without refreshment, and rode home several miles, thinly clad, in the evening, against a chilly south wind." Seriously ill, Percival was treated by Dr. J. L. Jenckes, who moved him into his own home to care for him. He stayed with Jenckes for three weeks, recovering his health completely and in the process gaining a devoted friend.

By the middle of November, Percival was able to return to work and began traveling extensively with Warner. He gave an account of the prairie fires they had encountered, which were a unique phenomenon for him:

> We started so late yesterday that we rode some part of the way, and the air was so smoky from prairie fires that I could see but a short distance. We, however, crossed some extensive, open, rolling prairies, of rich black soil, a considerable part ebony black from recent fires, the rest brown, and stripped of the splendid robe of golden and purple flowers which covered them through the summer and early autumn. As we approached this place we had a brilliant view of two extensive fires, one advancing on the prairie in a line of one to two miles,—slowly before a fresh west wind, in a front of detached dancing flames, with open intervals, like the squadrons of an army, leaving a black waste behind them; the other climbing the southwest slope of the northwest Platte Mound close by here, in the same detached manner from base to summit; both after dark rising with increased splendor, and throwing on the hazy sky a mimic aurora with the same black arch below that we see in the real aurora.[12]

Percival then prepared his report for the American Mining Company, concluding that there were "good lead bearing rocks" extending several hundred feet below ground. He recommended that the company drive shafts and use pumps to drain the water. As a result, the American Mining Company hired fifty men and built at its Playfair Mine several buildings, including an engine house for pumping water and a machine shop. Apparently Percival was right, and the value of the mining region increased "at least a million dollars." Pleased with the results, Percival wrote to Herrick, "I have found something new and peculiar in every mine I have entered; and yet all conform to one general law—unity with great variety."[13] Even in his report to the American Mining Company, Percival's insistence on perfection came through. Apparently he first gave the report to Warner, who suggested that a single word be changed. "Percival insisted upon the correctness of the word as he had used it. Remonstrance proved unavailing. The definitions of words and their proper use in sentences were to him positive things, and, after writing an important document, he could not admit it contained mistakes."[14]

On the basis of his successful work for the American Mining Company, Percival was asked by William A. Barstow, the governor of Wisconsin, to undertake a statewide survey as he had done for Connecticut.[15] On August 12, 1854, he was appointed state geologist of Wisconsin, replacing Edward Daniels, who had already been appointed and had completed some preliminary work. Daniels had little geological experience and the mine owners were dissatisfied. Nevertheless, his dismissal stirred up turmoil among legislators and the press in Madison, the state capital, making Percival hesitate to take the position. Apparently Daniels himself encouraged Percival to accept. Not until six months later, in February 1855, when the first interim report was released, did the criticism of Percival's appointment die down. That month, the *Weekly Argus* proclaimed, "Dr. Percival is a man whose scientific and professional reputation is genuine and current. His favorable opinion upon the subject of our mineral resources is itself money in our pockets. Moneyed men have that confidence in the result of his investigation that they will invest thousands of capital on the mere strength of that alone. He is a man of venerable years, whose complete and extensive acquaintance with science and whose fame as a practical geologist should be his security from attacks."[16]

With his appointment as state geologist, Percival now had all
Wisconsin spread out before him, not just the lead mines in the
southwest corner of the state. For the first time, Percival saw prai-
ries that extended from horizon to horizon, where the wind never
stopped rippling through the tall grasses. When he knelt down to
dig up a sample of soil, he found it dark and rich, presaging a future as farmland. His trips took him through forests so vast and
difficult to traverse he could travel twenty miles without seeing
a house. To his assessments of lead, he added zinc, copper, and
iron and then explained the occurrence of limestone, magnesium,
sandstone, and blue shale. By the beginning of 1855, Percival had
traveled approximately six thousand miles and examined more
than two hundred mines and quarries with names such as Buz-
zard's Roost Diggings, Peddler Creek, and Diamond Grove.[17]

Then, too, he had come across several geological puzzles that
begged for explanation. One would eventually be known as the
driftless zone, meaning that there was no glacial drift (till) deposited as a glacier retreated. Instead of clay, sand, and gravel, the
driftless zone was steep and rocky with carved-out valleys pocked
with caves and sinkholes. Percival noted the lack of glacial drift
and speculated that the escarpment and high ridges perhaps ob-
structed the course of "drift current."[18] The mounds were another
puzzle. They were lone rocky summits (also called monadnocks)
that reared up disconnectedly from the prairie. Because the American Mining Company was operating near the Sinsinawa mound,
Percival had begun his exploration there, finding it consisted of
distinct limestone beds "fine grained and nearly white" without
any evidence of lead, although he saw signs of "fruitless excava-
tions" made by out-of-luck prospectors.[19]

When he was not descending by ladder into the total black-
ness of mines with only a flickering lamp to illuminate the seams
and his hammer to chip out samples (suffering a few accidents
along the way, which he mentioned without detail in his letters),
he spent time on the surface with the miners and their families,
indulging in his second intellectual pastime, comparative linguis-
tics. According to Horace Rublee, whose home Percival occasionally
visited, Percival could converse fluently with the miners no mat-

ter the language, the possible exception being Gaelic and Cornish spoken by the men from Ireland and Cornwall. Percival had studied both Gaelic and Welsh, which is related to Cornish, so while he was not fluent, he was capable of understanding the oddities of the language and found it fascinating.[20]

However, Percival was most intrigued by the languages and cultures of the Native Americans he encountered during his travels. Connecticut had only a few Indians left, who lived in small family units usually on marginal land in poverty. The intact and robust cultures of the Winnebago (Ho-Chunk) and Chippewa (Ojibwa) were eye-opening to Percival, although it was already clear they were under extreme threat from Indian removal laws as more and more whites moved west and demanded the tribes be driven from their lands. In fact, the Winnebago war of 1827 (actually more of a skirmish) was caused by lead miners staking claims on Indian land and refusing to leave. Percival spent time with the Winnebago and Chippewa, sitting with them outside their domed shelters, listening intently. He was made to feel welcome most likely because he had not come to trade but to learn. As Jenckes, Percival's physician and friend, recalled, "Alone in the forest with the red men, who were always friendly to him, he succeeded in learning something of their language and history. The language of the Chippewas he considered euphonious, that of the Winnebagoes, harsh and guttural. Yet, from his slight investigations of their two dialects, he thought they originally spoke one language."[21]

While his interest in languages remained strong, Percival turned away from poetry entirely except for the poem "The German Patriot," which he wrote in German for a club in Madison that had requested it for their journal *Staats-Zeitung*. Percival told Lyman Draper, an historian with whom he often visited when in Madison, that he regretted ever having published poetry because some people claimed he was "nothing but a madcap poet" and therefore did not take him seriously. He considered his life a failure because he could have accomplished much more if he had devoted himself to science. Even so, people sometimes expected him to fill the role of poet and were surprised when he refused. For example, on a visit to River Falls, his hosts took him to the waterfalls expecting him to wax poetic at its beauty; instead he got busy with his hammer, taking a sample of the rock.[22] There is one more story worth telling. One evening, Percival stopped at a rough-hewn cabin on the frontier seeking lodging for the night. On entering the house and introducing himself, he was asked by one of the children if he were the poet. When he replied affirmatively, the child stood up tall and recited one of Percival's poems that he had memorized for school. The unexpectedness of the recitation in a lonely place touched Percival deeply.[23]

On his travels, Percival was often surprised at the difference between the settled eastern states and the territories. Because Wisconsin had become a state only seven years before, in 1848, it was in great flux. The population had risen sharply as people from New England as well as Norwegians and Germans had flooded in, some to settle, others to move through on their way to lands further west. In a letter written from Iowa County, Wisconsin, dated May 28, 1855, Percival remarked on the shifting population:

> There is a very great emigration this year to the Northwest and West. I have crossed the state this spring from Hartford, Washington County, to the southwest corner and on every main road leading north and west have been found a constant stream of emigrants. I have passed several trains of ten to twelve wagons with droves of cattle by the hundred. I met one train of twelve wagons from the town of Deane, Dane County, with nearly three hundred cattle going to Minnesota to squat as preemptioners on the St. Peter's River. The Norwegians are leaving in great numbers for that part. They leave their little improvements of forty acres to take up large tracts out west. Emigrants are coming in from the East to supply the place of the emigrants from this state.[24]

As he had done with his Connecticut survey, Percival wrote the first report from memory. Edward M. Hunter, who was the private secretary to Governor Barstow and who came to know Percival very well, recalled that "a small room had been partitioned off for his use, over a building erected for the storing of wood in the rear of the capitol. . . . Here, with no other materials than pen, ink, and paper, he wrote out from memory the Report I have mentioned. Should you give a condensed statement of what is contained in this Report, it will be difficult for your readers to realize how any man could retain in his memory the vast amount of material he has so luminously placed upon record."[25]

A peculiar friendship developed between Hunter and Percival, who would occasionally enter Hunter's office when Hunter was alone and would begin talking nonstop, "holding me a willing captive, perfectly enchanted, until some one would dissolve the spell by entering the room, when the Doctor would drop his head, become instantly silent, and glide away." Once Hunter had received some samples of iron ore from near Lake Superior, which were sitting on his desk. On seeing them, Percival commenced explaining about iron, telling Hunter, "In case you can secure any of this land, Mr. Hunter, I would advise you to do so. This ore is as much or better than the best Norway ore as that is superior to the common New Jersey." Hunter did not take his advice, which he came to regret.[26]

Hunter also related a humorous story about Percival's interactions with an assistant who had been assigned by Governor Barstow to help him with the survey, protect him from robbers, and perhaps hurry him along. Usually Percival traveled alone as he had done in Connecticut, although he had consented to traveling by horse and buggy instead of walking. When the assistant was unable to join Percival, he sent his seventeen-year-old son in his place. About two weeks later, Percival showed up at Hunter's office in a huff, telling him that the young man annoyed him exceedingly. When Hunter inquired what was the matter, Percival exclaimed, "Sir, he *whistles, he throws stones at birds, and he speaks to people with whom we meet on the road*: indeed, I cannot go with him any longer." And so the young man was let go and Percival returned to his lonely ways.[27]

In the introductory statement to the report addressed to Governor Barstow, Percival wrote, "One of the most important objects of a geological survey, indeed the most important, is to determine the system of arrangement, and the principles connected therewith, which may serve as a guide through what would be other-wise an inextricable labyrinth."[28] This sounded much like his claim to Governor Edwards in Connecticut that determining the system of traprock was what mattered, not simply naming the minerals. The report was in some ways a textbook, stressing above all the importance of understanding stratification so as to be able to find ore. It was critical for miners to know "that different rocks have different relations to particular minerals; that a given metallic vein in one stratum, will yield more abundantly than in another, and will present peculiar characters in traversing each stratum." By learning about stratification, "a miner will know what depth of mineral-bearing rock he may there expect, how many open-ings and of what character he may reasonably expect to meet." Such knowledge would give to mining and prospecting "a degree of certainty."[29]

Percival was concerned that most of the mines were too shal-low, on average thirty to forty feet, and needed to be much deeper, with attention paid to the pumping of water. "As little has been done in deep mining, and the deepest shafts yet sunk have been abandoned," he wrote, "I have had fewer opportunities than I could wish of tracing the mineral at the same point through different strata."[30]

One of his most important recommendations was that for min-ing to be economically successful, legislators and mine owners had to consider the need for fuel and transportation from the mines to the manufacturers, not just the existence of ore. Instead of ox-teams slowly hauling heavy wagons on poor roads, Percival recom-mended a railroad connection be built between coal needed for the smelting furnaces and zinc ores, which he considered abundant and a possible source of profit. "Either the fuel might be taken to the ore, or the ore to the fuel, as should be found most advanta-geous," he wrote. "Other routes of communication would soon be opened, and thus, with American skill and enterprise, a new min-ing interest would be created, which would compare favorably with the present." Percival also prepared the *Report on the iron of Dodge and Washington counties, State of Wisconsin*, in which he expressed optimism about the ore at a place called Iron Ridge, in the southeast corner. As a result, the *Milwaukee Daily News* ran an article on May 22, 1855, complimenting Percival's work and encouraging investment in iron mining.[31]

In the late winter and early spring of 1855, after the first reports were published, Percival returned to New Haven just long enough to move his possessions from his apartment in the empty hospital to a new home of his own (see plate 14). Intending to return to the city permanently after his work in Wisconsin was done, Percival had arranged to buy a plot of land on Park Place on which to build a simple structure where he could retire in comfort and seclusion. He was fifty-nine years old and was beginning to feel the pull of years. With his friend Edward Herrick spearheading the project, a one-story house was built in his absence. Similar to a hermitage, it was mainly a library and study with no front door, only a back one. Narrow windows were placed high in the front wall to allow in light but not the gaze of people passing by. Nathaniel Parker Willis likened the new house to "a sarcophagus in a cathedral aisle." In hyperbolic language, Willis wrote that it was a place for the purest of geniuses: "profound science and lofty poetry straining his soul to the two extremes of a seraph's span, with scarcely mortality enough to keep him down to the ground." Completed in November 1854, the house stood empty until Percival's arrival three months later. Once the move of his library, rock collection, and furniture was completed, Percival closed up the house and returned to Wisconsin. Although he was looking forward to returning to his new home, he was tempted to stay in Hazel Green and even considered purchasing a small farm where he could have a garden and live at peace surrounded by his books. He shared his ideas with Dr. Jenckes, telling him in 1856 that his time in Wisconsin "was the happiest three years of his life."[32]

The rest of 1855 was filled with intense work. Unfortunately, payment from the State of Wisconsin was sporadic, forcing Percival to cover expenses and wondering whether it would be better to work for mining companies, where politics did not play a part. Percival wrote to Henry White, a state official, on December 10, 1855, about the travel he had done in preparation for the second report:

After I wrote you I made a journey through the western counties of the state as far as the Falls of the St. Croix, Polk County, and returned part of the way through Minnesota. In the course of my tour I visited twelve counties in Wisconsin, which I had not before visited, and seven in Minnesota. I returned to Hazel Green November 2 and after a short rest proceeded on a tour through eight of the southern counties and arrived at Madison December 2. I have now visited to a greater or less extent 38 of the 50 counties in the state and, besides a particular examination of the lead mines, have made a general reconnaissance of all the southern and more settled parts of the state.

He then wrote that his "journey to the northwest was very difficult from bad roads and the unsettled state of the country. I crossed two tracts of twenty miles without inhabitants, one alone across a prairie; one (with a companion recommended to me) through a heavy timber country. It was fortunate he accompanied me, as I got badly stuck half way and could not have extricated myself alone. Several other accidents of a similar kind have occurred to me, but fortunately within a short distance of help."[33]

Shortly after his letter to White, Percival fell seriously ill due to extensive travel in severe weather. Again he came under the solicitous care of his friend Dr. Jenckes, who found it difficult to make a diagnosis and to provide relief. Over the next few months, Percival became emaciated and listless. Several times he told Jenckes, "Since living at the West, I have overtasked my physical strength, and I feel that I am worn out." Yet he continued to make an effort to complete the second report. In his last letter to Governor Barstow, dated March 10, 1856, Percival wrote, "My health is very bad, nor am I able to attend to my report, nor can I promise when I shall be able to prepare it."[34] When Dr. Jenckes raised the subject of his dying and where he would like to be buried, Jenckes assumed he would say New Haven, but Percival replied, "I wish to be buried here, and let my remains be undisturbed." To provide better medical care, Jenckes moved him into his own home as he had done during Percival's previous illness. There Percival died on May 2,

1856, "surrounded by kind friends, who tenderly and affectionately ministered to his temporal wants, and closed his eyes forever at the dawn of the day, as the sun was just rising and threw a flood of golden light over the scene."[35]

Dr. Jenckes wrote that Percival was never a cynic or a misanthrope. In fact, during his time in Hazel Green he had come to enjoy the presence of children—who affectionately called him the Old Stone Breaker—taking them for buggy rides. Referring to Percival's friends back in Connecticut, Jenckes wrote, "It would have rejoiced his friends could they have seen him at this time. Translated from the isolation of a lonely room to the happy influences of a home, free from the immediate pressure of pecuniary want, surrounded by little children and a circle of friends by whom he was appreciated, but few would have recognized in the active, energetic, and social man the reserved Percival of other years."[36]

The second part of Percival's report was published in 1856 following his death. The reaction was mixed. Legislators and miners wanted a report that showed, like an X on a treasure map, where minerals were located so they could be dug up. They did not want a lecture on strata. Yet there were many people who saw value in his work and remembered Percival fondly. Many years after his death, a group of Connecticut citizens paid for a grave marker in which were cut the following words: "Eminent As A Poet, Rarely Accomplished As A Linguist, Learned And Acute in Science, A Man Without Guile."

Epilogue

Percival longed to be a normal human being with friends, a home of his own, and the respect of his peers. By the end of his life he had attained all three, although he never lived in the house built for him in New Haven. Even so, his prodigious intellect and mental illness imposed heavy burdens on him, foremost among them being loneliness. He was at heart a kind and sensitive man who struggled to express his feelings toward others in socially acceptable ways. Fortunately, some of his friends considered his awkward efforts endearing. Samuel Griswold Goodrich told a story in his memoirs about an incident that occurred at the time Goodrich embarked for Europe. Percival had accompanied him to the *Canada*, anchored in the Hudson River, and then had abruptly said goodbye. Much later, after Goodrich had arrived in London, he was reading a New York newspaper only to find in its pages a beautiful poem titled "To the *Canada* on Going to Sea," signed with a *P*. "I knew Percival too well to feel hurt at his cold good-bye," Goodrich wrote, "nevertheless, it was a pleasure to have this evidence of his feeling and friendship."[1]

As to Percival's poetry, by the 1830s it was out of fashion. After his death, his friends helped to arrange for a handsome two-volume publication titled *The Poetical Works of James Gates Percival*. Edited by Lucius W. Fitch, it was published by Ticknor and Fields in 1859 and was part of their Blue and Gold series, which included the works of Henry Wadsworth Longfellow and Oliver Wendell

Holmes. In the *Evening Post*, William Cullen Bryant wrote, "Those who look over these volumes will, we think, wonder that poems which gave so much delight when they first appeared have been so much neglected since, and will be glad of the opportunity of renewing their acquaintance with an author who, while he was one of the most learned of poets, was also one of the most spontaneous in the manifestations of genius."[2] Not all the reviewers of *The Poetical Works* were so kind. James Russell Lowell wrote a screed that was brutal, mocking Percival for the mental illness that doomed him to defeat, as shown in his inability to edit and sharpen his work. "His verse carries every inch of canvas that diction and sentiment can crowd, but the craft is cranky, and we miss the deep-grasping keel of reason, which alone can steady and give direction. His mind drifts, too waterlogged to answer the helm."[3] Lowell's overblown attack shredded any chance of future appreciation of Percival's poetry. By the twentieth century his poems were no longer anthologized, the only exception being "The Coral Grove." In his essay "The Limits of Recovery: The Failure of James Gates Percival," John Hay, associate professor of English at the University of Nevada, Las Vegas, wrote that Percival's downfall was "a very real transition from national literary eminence to popular and widespread indifference of a rapidity that perplexed even his contemporaries." Partially because of the negative reviews as well as his writing style, Percival became "a dead end" for literary scholars, a fact that remains the case today even though his work is available on the internet.[4]

In the sphere of geology, Percival's impact was large while his fame was small. (See plate 15.) However, it must be recognized that fame came to relatively few geologists no matter their contribution to knowledge. The geologist James Dana (whose fame was also fleeting) readily gave Percival credit for his ideas on the nature of traprock and the upwelling of magma through fissures. Percival's careful observations provided evidence of an ancient earth where monumental events, both fast and slow, utterly changed the landscape. Percival did not know of plate tectonics, but he intuited that what he discerned in Connecticut went far beyond state lines, stretching at least from the Watchung Mountains and Palisades all the way up to the Bay of Fundy. Moreover, the past was not past. What was to prevent magma from rising up again and breaking through the surface as lava? The fact that there was no sign of a recent occurrence was no guarantee it could not happen again.

In his insightful book *Geology in the Nineteenth Century: Changing Views of a Changing World*, Mott Greene wrote, "Every major controversy had but a single outcome; geology was a larger and more difficult enterprise than had previously been imagined. Unlike those disciplines that in their best moments seem to converge toward fundamentals, geology was constantly faced with dispersive tasks." For instance, the study of how rocks were formed led to the study of how mountain ranges were formed (a preoccupation in the nineteenth century), which led to the study of how continents were formed. Along the way, many outrageous speculations were made that did not rise to the level of hypotheses and theories. And yet geology advanced anyway. Greene concluded, "To my knowledge, no one has yet studied the possibility that a science might advance vigorously in the face of general and even cheerful agreement that no adequate comprehensive theory exists."[5]

I began this book by mentioning the two rocks that sit on my desk: the first is iron slag and the second is columnar traprock from the Hanging Hills. I have another piece of traprock that I picked up from Ragged Mountain to the west of Percival's home in Kensington. The weathered exterior is reddish brown and the interior is dark grey. It is not hexagonal. It comes from the top layer of the Holyoke Basalt flow, which is approximately four hundred feet thick. The lower layers of the flow are highly fractured, but the upper layers provide some of the best, and safest, rock climbing in New England.[6] It is likely that Percival climbed Ragged Mountain. I can see him taking out his hammer and chisel and chipping off a specimen from the cliff face, holding it in his hand and studying it closely to understand why it differed from other traprock in the region. Refusing to speculate about its age, he would have asked instead if it had it been made by fire, to which his answer would have been yes. Then he would have wondered if chemical composition and the way it had cooled played a role. As he had written to Edward Hitchcock, the business of a geologist was not to determine how the earth *was* made but "how the earth *is* made, or at least that part of it within the limits of our observation." To Percival, the *making* of the earth was ongoing, ever changing, and far beyond a human being's ability to fully understand.

Selected Poetry of James Gates Percival

The following poems are found in *The Poetical Works of James Gates Percival*, a two-volume set published after Percival's death.

THE CORAL GROVE

Deep in the wave is a coral grove,
Where the purple mullet, and gold-fish rove,
Where the sea-flower spreads its leaves of blue,
That never are wet with falling dew,
But in bright and changeful beauty shine,
Far down in the green and glassy brine.
The floor is of sand, like the mountain drift,
And the pearl-shells spangle the flinty snow;
From coral rocks the sea plants lift
Their boughs, where the tides and billows flow;
The water is calm and still below,
For the winds and waves are absent there,
And the sands are bright as the stars that glow
In the motionless fields of upper air:
There with its waving blade of green,
The sea-flag streams through the silent water,
And the crimson leaf of the dulse is seen
To blush, like a banner bathed in slaughter:
There with a light and easy motion,
The fan-coral sweeps through the clear, deep sea;

And the yellow and scarlet tufts of ocean
Are bending like corn on the upland lea:
And life, in rare and beautiful forms,
Is sporting amid those bowers of stone,
And is safe, when the wrathful spirit of storms,
Has made the top of the waves his own:
And when the ship from his fury flies,
Where the myriad voices of ocean roar,
When the wind-god frowns in the murky skies,
And demons are waiting the wreck on shore;
Then far below in the peaceful sea,
The purple mullet, and gold-fish rove,
Where the waters murmur tranquilly,
Through the bending twigs of the coral grove.

FROM POETRY

   'Tis not the chime and flow of words, that move
In measured file, and metrical array;
'Tis not the union of returning sounds,
Nor all the pleasing artifice of rhyme,
And quantity, and accent, that can give
This all-pervading spirit to the ear,
Or blend it with the movings of the soul.
'Tis a mysterious feeling, which combines
Man with the world around him, in a chain
Woven of flowers, and dipped in sweetness, till
He taste the high communion of his thoughts,
With all existences, in earth and heaven,
That meet him in the charm of grace and power.
'Tis not the noisy babbler, who displays,
In studied phrase, and ornate epithet,
And rounded period, poor and vapid thoughts,
Which peep from out the cumbrous ornaments
That overload their littleness. Its words
Are few, but deep and solemn; and they break
Fresh from the fount of feeling, and are full

Of all that passion, which, on Carmel, fired
The holy prophet, when his lips were coals,
His language winged with terror, as when bolts
Leap from the brooding tempest, armed with wrath
Commissioned to affright us, and destroy.

XXXIV (FROM PROMETHEUS)

This is the old age of our fallen race;
We mince in steps correct, but feeble; creep
By rule unwavering in a tortoise pace;
We do not, like the new-born ancient, leap
At once o're mind's old barriers, but we keep
Drilling and shaving down the wall; we play
With stones and shells and flowers, and as we peep
In nature's outward folds, like infants, say,
How bright and clear and pure our intellectual day.

LXIII (FROM PROMETHEUS)

Nature! When looking on thee, I become
Renewed to my first being, and am pure,
As thou art bright and lovely; from the hum
Of cities, where men linger and endure
That wasting death, which kills them with a sure
But long-felt torture, I now haste away
To climb thy rugged rocks, and find the cure
Of all my evils, and again be gay
In the clear sun, that gilds the fair autumnal day.

LXVI (FROM PROMETHEUS)

But Nature! thou hast more beneath me bright
In their rich autumnal tints, than all I throw
Over the crystal arch, whose tranquil light
Takes every hue of mellowness below;
It kindles in the orchard's ruddy glow,

And on the colored woods, whose dying shade
Crowns the tall mountain with a wreath, whose flow,
Softly descending to the silent glade,
Seems like the evening cloud in airy tints arrayed.

LXXIX (*FROM PROMETHEUS*)

The gray rocks, and the mountains wrapped in blue,
Towering far distant through the silent air,
That sleeps in noon-light, but in morning blew
Fresh o'er the russet plain, and scattered there
Shadows from flitting clouds, that earth seemed fair
Robed in a sheet of light, and then grew dim;—
Far distant through the haze, those mountains bear
Sky-lifted walls, that frown along the brim
Of earth, and, as I gaze, in vapor seem to swim.

CXXVI (*FROM PROMETHEUS*)

The clouds are thine, and all their magic hues
Are penciled by thee; when thou bendest low,
Or comest in thy strength, thy hand imbues
Their waving fold with such a perfect glow
Of all pure tints, the fairy pictures throw
Shame on the proudest art,—the tender stain
Hung round the verge of heaven, that as a bow
Girds the wide world, and in their blended chain
All tints to the deep gold, that flashes in thy train—

CLI (*FROM PROMETHEUS*)

We would be gods, and we would know all things,
And therefore we know nothing well; our thought
Would lift itself on eagle's wings,
And speed through all that Deity hath wrought
And fashioned by his fiat, until naught

Should be untraveled, but the aspiring flame
Consumes the active mind, and all it sought
Becomes its torment, for the breath of fame,
Like a Sirocco's blast, will sear and scorch our frame.

CXCIX (*FROM PROMETHEUS*)

'Tis not for me,—I am of sterner mould;
I must live in my own heart, and find
Strength to sustain—by thought; my only hold
Is on that unbent energy of mind,
Which, as the storm beats harder on, will bind
Closer its will around it, and endure;
Which shuns all concord with its own base kind,
Where it for ever totters, but grows pure
And firm in solitude, which is its only cure.

SONNET

FAREWELL! Ye visions of my wayward brain,
Farewell! I send you from this lonely bower;
But I shall ne'er forget your soothing power,
Although perhaps we never meet again;
Yet I have not communed with you in vain,
If but some portion of that hallowed fire,
Which roused the ancient bard to pour his strain,
Has warmed my lips and raised my spirit higher.
Ye go abroad upon a stormy sea,
But there are some, perchance, may not despise
Such trifles, though they were composed by me,
And they may view them with approving eyes
While I, as I have ever been, shall be,
Lone reader of the woods, the waters, and the skies.

SONNET VII, NIGHT

Am I not all alone?—The world is still
In passionless slumber,—not a tree but feels
The far-pervading hush, and softer steals
The misty river by. Yon broad bare hill
Looks coldly up to heaven, and all the stars
Seem eyes deep fixed in silence, as if bound
By some unearthly spell,—no other sound
But the owl's unfrequent moan.—Their airy cars
The winds have stationed on the mountain peaks.
Am I not all alone?—A spirit speaks
From the abyss of night, "Not all alone,—
Nature is round thee with her banded powers,
And ancient genius haunts thee in these hours;—
Mind and its kingdom now are all thine own."

SONNET IX

Whence? Whither? Where?—A taper point of light,
   My life and world—the infinite around;
   A sea, not even highest thought can sound;
A formless void; unchanging, endless night.

In vain the struggling spirit aims its flight
   To the empyrean, seen as is a star,
   Sole glimmering through the hazy night afar,—
In vain it beats its wings with daring might.

What yonder gleams? What heavenly shapes arise
   From out the bodiless waste? Behold the dawn,
   Sent from on high! Uncounted ages gone,
Burst full and glorious on my wondering eyes:
   Sun-clear the world around, and far away,
   A boundless future sweeps in golden day.

SONNET II

O Evening! I have loved thee with a joy
Tender and pure, and thou hast ever been
A soother of my sorrows. When a boy,
I wandered often to a lonely glen,
And, far from all the stir and noise of men,
Held fond communion with unearthly things
Such as come gathering brightly round us, when
Imagination soars and shakes her wings.

Yes, in the secret valley, double dear
For all its natural beauty, and the hush
That ever brooded o'er it, I would lay
My thought in deepest calm, and if a bush
Rustled, or small bird shook the beechen spray,
There seemed a ministering angel whispering near.

THE DESERTED WIFE

He comes not;—I have watched the moon go down,
But yet he comes not. Once it was not so.
He thinks not how these bitter tears do flow,
The while he holds his riot in that town.
Yet he will come, and chide, and I shall weep;
And he will wake my infant from its sleep,
To blend its feeble wailing with my tears.
O, how I love a mother's watch to keep,
Over those sleeping eyes, that smile, which cheers
My heart, though sunk in sorrow, fixed and deep!
I had a husband, once, who loved me,—now,
He ever wears a frown upon his brow,
And feeds his passion on a wanton's lip,
As bees, from laurel flowers, a poison sip;
But yet I cannot hate.—O, there were hours
When I could hang forever on his eye,
And Time, who stole with silent swiftness by,

Strewed, as he hurried on, his path with flowers.
I loved him then,—he loved me too. My heart
Still finds its fondness kindle, if he smile;
The memory of our loves will ne'er depart;
And though he often sting me with a dart,
Venomed and barbed, and waste upon the vile
Caresses which his babe and mine should share,
Though he should spurn me, I will calmly bear
His madness,—and should sickness come, and lay
Its paralyzing hand upon him, then
I would with kindness all my wrongs repay,
Until the penitent should weep, and say
How injured, and how faithful, I had been.

SENECA LAKE

One evening in the pleasant month of May,
On a green hillock swelling from the shore
Above thy emerald wave, when the clear west
Was all one sheet of light, I sat me down,
Wearied, yet happy. I had wandered long,
That bright, fair day; and all the way my path
Was tended by a warm and soothing air,
That breathed like bliss; and round me all the woods
Opened their yellow buds, and every cottage
Was bowered in blossoms, for the orchard trees
Were all in flower. I came at close of day,
Down to thy brink, and it was pleasure there
To bathe my dripping forehead in thy cool,
Transparent waters. I refreshed me long
With the bright sparkling stream, and from the pebbles,
That bedded all thy margin, singled out
Rare casts of unknown shells, from off thy cliffs
Broken by wintry surges. Thou wert calm,
Even as an infant calm, that gentle evening;
And one could hardly dream thou 'dst ever met
And wrestled with the storm. A breath of air,

Felt only in its coolness, from the west
Stole over thee, and stirred thy golden mirror
Into long waves, that only showed themselves
In ripples on thy shore,—far distant ripples,
Breaking the silence with their quiet kisses,
And softly murmuring peace. Up the green hillock
I mounted languidly, and at the summit
On the new grass reposed, and saw that evening
Fade sweetly over thee.
                        Far to the south
Thy slumbering waters floated, one long sheet
Of burnished gold,—between thy nearer shores
Softly embraced, and melting distantly
Into a yellow haze, embosomed low
'Mid shadowy hills and misty mountains, all
Covered with showery light, as with a veil
Of airy gauze. Beautiful were thy shores,
And manifold their outlines, here up-swelling
In bossy green,—there hung in slaty cliffs,
Black as if hewn from jet, and overtopped
With the dark cedar's tufts, or new-leaved birch,
Bright as the wave below. How glassy clear
The far expanse! Beneath it all the sky
Swelled downward, and its fleecy clouds were gay
With all their rainbow fringes, and the trees
And cliffs and grassy knolls were all repeated
Along the uncertain shores,—so clearly seen
Beneath the invisible transparency,
That land and water mingled, and the one
Seemed melting in the other. O, how soft
Yon mountain's heavenly blue, and all o'erlaid
With a pale tint of roses! Deep between
The ever-narrowing lake, just faintly marked
By its reflected light, and farther on
Buried in vapory foam, as if a surf
Heaved on its utmost shore. How deep the silence!
Only the rustling boughs, the broken ripple,

The cricket and the tree-frog, with the tinkle
Of bells in fold and pasture, or a voice
Heard from a distant farm, or hollow bay
Of home-returning hound,—a virgin land
Just rescued from the wilderness, still showing
Wrecks of the giant forest, yet all bright
With a luxuriant culture, springing wheat,
And meadows richly green,—the blessed gift
Of liberty and law. I gazed upon them,
And on the unchanging lake, and felt awhile
Unutterable joy,—I loved my land
With more than filial love,—it was a joy
That only spake in tears.
                    With early dawn
I woke, and found the lake was up before me,
For a fresh, stirring breeze came from the south,
And all its deep-green waves were tossed and mingled
Into a war of foam. The new-risen sun
Shone on them, as if they were worlds of stars,
Or gems, or crystals, or some other thing
Sparry and flashing bright. A gentle murmur,
A roar scarce uttered, like a voice of mirth
Amid the dancing waters, blended well
With the Æolian whispering of boughs
In a wide grove of pines. The fields and woods
Were sparkling all with dew, and curling smoke
Rose from the cottage fires;—the robin, too,
And the brown thrush, and other birds concealed
Amid the half-blown thickets, joyously
Poured out their morning songs, and thus attended,
I wandered by the shore. O, it was pleasant
To feel the dashing of the dewy spray
Rain on my forehead, and to look between
Long crests of foam, into an unknown depth
Of deepest green, and then to see that green
Soft changing into snow. Over this waste
Of rolling surges, on a lofty bank

With a broad surf beneath it, brightly shone
White roofs and spires, and gilded vanes, and windows,
Each like a flame,—thy peaceful tenements,
Geneva, aptly named; for not the walls
By the blue, arrowy Rhone, nor Leman's lake,
With all its vineyard shores and mouldering castles,
Nor even its shaggy mountains, nor above
Its world of Alpine snows,—these are not more
Than thou, bright Seneca, whether at peace,
As I at evening met thee, or this morning,
Tossed into foam. Thou too shalt have thy fame:
Genius shall make thy hills his home, and here
Shall build his airy visions,—bards shall come,
And fondly sing thee,—pilgrims too shall haunt
Thy sacred waters, and in after ages,
O, may some votary sit on the hillock,
At evening, by thy shore!

THE DEATH OF A CHILD

I sat beside the pillow of a child,—
His dying pillow,—and I watched the ebb
Of his last fluttering breath. All tranquilly
He passed away, and not a murmur came
From his white lips. A film crept o'er his eye,
But did not all conceal it, and at times
The darkness stole away, and he looked out
Serenely, with an innocent smile, as if
Pleased with an infant's toy; and there was then
A very delicate flush upon his cheek,
Like the new edging of a damask-rose,
When first the bud uncloses. As I watched,
I caught at these awakenings better hope,
And, yielding to the longing of my heart,
Fancied I saw him opening from a trance,
And with a gentle effort shaking off
The oppression of a dream. A moment more,

And the film mantled o'er his eye again,
And the faint redness left his faltering lips,
And backward to its centre in the heart
The crimson current rallied, leaving him
Like a chill statue, icy cold and pale.
He was my only one, and I had long
Loved him for all his innocent playfulness,
And his endearing fondness. He would hang
Whole days around me, watching all I did,
And questioning each particular act, as if
He could not rest till he had known the why
Of every word and motion. I indulged him,
And in that kind of indulgence found his love
Grow every hour till I was as his life,
And he was more than mine. Well pleased I saw
His opening faculties, and well I knew
His curious bent betokened better things
In a maturer age; but when he seemed
Rosy, and full of health, and o'er-informed
With life's young buoyancy, a hidden blight
Nipped him, and he decayed. He sank away
With scarce a visible token, like a breath
Of summer wind, when it has spent itself,
And blows so faintly, that the feathery leaves
Of the mimosa only tell of it,
All others resting as if nothing stirred
In the wide air. I watched him eagerly,
And I could only see that he decayed,
And soon must die. With a consenting stillness
My heart grew calm, and while his dying breath
Stole from his lips so faintly, not a murmur
Met the deep listening ear; I felt a power,
Too peaceful for an earthly emanation,
Come with a tranquillizing influence o'er me
And soothe me to the trial. As I looked,
The quivering of his lids, that lay like leaves
Of alabaster on his darkened eyes,

And the small trembling of his parted lips,
Curled outward like the margent of a lily,
Suddenly died away, and all was still.
Life was no more. I knew it, and at once
The utter loneliness of sorrow sank
Deep, deep within me, and awhile I sat
Without a tear. The stream was frozen up
And would not flow; but soon relenting nature
Gave way, and a full burst of passionate weeping
Flowed with a sudden gush, that quite unmanned me,
Then ebbing silently, it left me calm.

NIGHT WATCHING

She sat beside her lover, and her hand
Rested upon his clay-cold forehead. Death
Was calmly stealing o'er him, and his life
Went out by silent flickerings, when his eye
Woke up from its dim lethargy, and cast
Bright looks of fondness on her. He was weak,
Too weak to utter all his heart. His eye
Was now his only language, and it spake
How much he felt her kindness, and the love
That sat, when all had fled, beside him. Night
Was far upon its watches, and the voice
Of Nature had no sound. The pure blue sky
Was fair and lovely, and the many stars
Looked down in tranquil beauty on an earth
That smiled in sweetest summer. She looked out
Through the raised window, and the sheeted bay
Lay in a quiet sleep below, and shone
With the pale beam of midnight;—all was still,
And the white sail, that o'er the distant stream
Moved with so slow a pace, it seemed at rest,
Fixed in the glassy water, and with care
Shunned the dark den of pestilence, and stole
Fearfully from the tainted gale that breathed

Softly along the crisping wave,—that sail
Hung loosely on its yard, and, as it flapped,
Caught moving undulations from the light,
That silently came down, and gave the hills,
And spires, and walls, and roofs, a tint so pale,
Death seemed on all the landscape,—but so still,
Who would have thought that anything but peace
And beauty had a dwelling there! The world
Had gone, and life was not within those walls,
Only a few, who lingered faintly on,
Waiting the moment of departure; or
Sat tending at their pillows, with a love
So strong it mastered fear,—and they were few,
And she was one,—and in a lonely house,
Far from all sight and sound of living thing,
She watched the couch of him she loved and drew
Contagion from the lips that were to her
Still beautiful as roses, though so pale
They seemed like a thin snow-curl. All was still,
And even so deeply hushed, the low, faint breath
That trembling gasped away came through the night
As a loud sound of awe. She passed her hand
Over those quivering lips, that ever grew
Paler and colder, as the only sign
To tell her life still lingered;—it went out!
And her heart sank within her, when the last
Weak sigh of life was over, and the room
Seemed like a vaulted sepulcher, so lone
She dared not look around: and the light wind,
That played among the leaves and flowers that grew
Still freshly at her window, and waved back
The curtain with a rustling sound, to her,
In her intense abstraction, seemed the voice
Of a departed spirit. He she heard,
At least in fancy heard, a whisper breathe
Close at her ear, and tell her all was done,
And her fond loves were ended. She had watched

Until her love grew manly, and she checked
The tears that came to flow, and nerved her heart
To the last solemn duty. With a hand
That trembled not, she closed the fallen lid,
And pressed the lips, and gave them one long kiss;—
Then decently spread over all a shroud;
And sitting with a look of lingering love
Intense in tearless passion, rose at length,
And, pressing both her hands upon her brow,
Gave loose to all her gushing grief in showers,
Which, as a fountain sealed till it had swelled
To its last fullness, now gave way and flowed
In a deep stream of sorrow. She grew calm,
And, parting back the curtains, looked abroad
Upon the moonlight loveliness, all sunk
In one unbroken silence, save the moan
From the lone room of death, or the dull sound
Of the slow-moving hearse. The homes of men
Were now all desolate, and darkness there,
And solitude and silence took their seat
In the deserted streets, as if the wing
Of a destroying angel had gone by
And blasted all existence, and had changed
The gay, the busy, and the crowded mart
To one cold, speechless city of the dead!

The Art of Nelson Augustus Moore

Nelson Augustus Moore was born in 1824 in Kensington, a town he considered to be "one of the most picturesque places in New England." He lived in Kensington his entire life except for brief periods spent in his art studio in New York City or in Hartford, Connecticut, where he owned a daguerreotype photography business.[1]

The Percival and Moore families knew each other well. During the 1820s, the Moores lived in the house in which Percival's mother, Elizabeth Hart, grew up. Both families owned shares in various mills. In 1822, the Moores decided to expand their mill operations into grinding limestone from a nearby quarry to be used in the making of cement. They purchased the land to build a new dam from Oswin Percival.

Because James Gates Percival was a generation older than Nelson Augustus Moore, Moore perceived him as a revered elder who had won national fame as a poet. Moore wrote in an unpublished autobiography that "no more highly educated man has ever lived in this society" and that his uncle, who knew Percival well, considered him to be at the time of Percival's death "almost a sinless human being."[2] What connected the two men was the land itself. Both were entranced by the traprock ridges surrounded by verdant farmland, and they longed to convey that hard-soft beauty in poetry, art, and geology. Moore's son, Ethelbert, wrote in his memoir, *The Tenth Generation*, that his father's "outdoor painting gave him an intimate knowledge of nature in its many moods. His trained observation for so many years disclosed much that is closed to many." Apart from the mention of painting, that quote is also true of Percival.[3]

Moore's first realization that art was his calling came from a strange event. Milo Hotchkiss, a local painter, was commissioned to paint a memorial portrait of a child who had died—a common practice in the days before photography. Apparently Hotchkiss asked Moore, then eighteen years old, to hold the lamp for him while he worked. In so doing, Moore glimpsed his future. Subsequently he took lessons from Hotchkiss. Then, when he was twenty-two years old, Moore wrote to Asher B. Durand, one of the leaders of the Hudson River School of landscape painters, asking for advice on art lessons. Perhaps Moore was hoping Durand would offer to teach him. Instead, Durand recommended Thomas Seir Cummings, a portraitist and a painter of miniatures in New York City. Until then, Moore had spent his spare time drawing likenesses of the men who worked at the Berlin train station, where he was an agent, using the station attic as a makeshift studio. With the support of his family, Moore took Durand's advice and went to New York City to study with Cummings. Although he learned a great deal, he was nonplused by the endless copying of lithographs and plaster casts, which he described as "old heads, which will not be very nice to look at." He also studied for a while with Daniel Huntington, who gave his students "pretty free rein, letting us draw or paint whatever we chose." Huntington was known for his portraits, genre paintings, and landscapes in the style of the Hudson River School.

The best art teacher was New York City itself, providing Moore the opportunity to meet other artists and to view their paintings at public exhibitions or in the privacy of their studios. In 1848, he saw an exhibition of Thomas Cole's art and was captivated by the grandeur of *The Course of Empire*, a series that featured in the background a mountain that looked like the traprock. Cole was a friend of both Benjamin Silliman and his brother-in-law, Daniel Wadsworth, and had climbed the ridges with them, even painting Wadsworth's Monte Video built on top of Talcott Mountain.

Moore was impressed as well by the work of two young paint-ers from Connecticut: John F. Kensett, from Cheshire, and Fred-eric Edwin Church, from Hartford. Church was already the heir apparent to the first generation of Hudson River School artists and was working on his masterful painting *West Rock*. For all of them, geology had a place of prominence. As Durand wrote in his "Letters on Landscape," in the publication *The Crayon*, artists must paint a "truthful representation" of the natural world. In regard to geology "the elevations and depressions of the earth's surface . . . may not be changed in the least perceptible degree, most es-pecially the mountain and hill forms. On these God has set his signet, and Art may not remove it when the picture professes to represent the scene."[4]

Perhaps if Moore had remained in New York City, he would have become famous, but Kensington was like a magnet and he was like an iron filing. In 1850 he made up his mind to go home, writing to his family, "I shall try to get into the landscape line, for I am very partial to landscape painting, and Mr. [George] Inness, a landscape painter of excellent reputation, advises me to paint landscape." The decision to become a landscape painter based in Kensington had major ramifications. In the book *Nelson Augustus Moore*, Ellen Fletcher explained, "if he had stayed in New York, he would have made deep, personal sacrifices of daily closeness to home and family, and of vital proximity to the native landscape that sustained his professional existence."[5] However, by returning to Kensington, Moore cut himself off from collectors and patrons who could have provided financial support.

In 1853, Moore married Ann Maria Pickett of Morris, Connecti-cut. The couple had four children: Edwin Augustus, Ellen Maria, Ethelbert Allen, and Alanson Jasper Pickett. Because the income from painting was not sufficient to provide for his family, in 1854 Moore and his brother opened a daguerreotype business, first in New Britain and then in Hartford. By 1860 he was prosperous enough to build the Stone House in Kensington, where he lived the rest of his life. Constructed out of traprock held together by cement made by his family's limestone-grinding mill, it was one of

Fig. A.1. This family portrait by an unidentified photographer shows Nelson Augustus Moore, his wife Ann Maria, and their children on the porch of the Stone House. Courtesy of the Moore Picture Trust.

the first houses in the nation to use cement in domestic architecture. Like the region itself, the house had a hard and soft quality, with the dark rock and light-colored cement decorated with Victorian wood filigree.

The need to make a living was also the reason that Moore began to spend summers painting at Lake George in the Adirondacks, which had become a popular tourist destination and a watering hole for the wealthy—just the people who were willing to commission a painting of the lake in its cool pristine beauty. Moore loved the dramatic sweep and misty light of the region, but he was also pragmatic about it, writing that business was his main reason for returning for twenty-five summers. "Lake George was my most remunerative ground, as after a few years I became well known, and it had almost the attractiveness of a home for me."[6]

Nevertheless, it was Kensington that was the center of Moore's being, and the paintings of his homeland have a warmth lacking in those of Lake George. Unlike some of the Hudson River School artists, Moore was not trying to capture the essence of the sublime in which human beings were reduced to awed observers—a prime example being Cole's painting of the oxbow on the Connecticut River, in which he included himself as a small figure sitting high up on the western side of Mt. Holyoke watching an oncoming storm. Moore did not paint people who were overwhelmed by the grandeur of their world; they were simply a part of it, whether haying, strolling down a country lane, herding cows, or fishing in a pond. So also Moore's mountains did not loom menacingly but instead rose gently in the background, emphasizing a pastoral foreground of peace and plenty. Often Moore used a warm color palette that included burnt sienna and ochre, as if he were sensing a bounteous autumn day even when his subject matter was an apple tree blooming in spring. In some of his winter scenes he used a soft yellow in the late day sky that was reflected on the ice across which skaters glided. This colorful vitality is in contrast to his use of subdued blues and grays in his Lake George paintings, where the people (often in boats) are tiny focal points in a vast remoteness instead of an integral part of the environment.

Moore wrote that a painting must convey to a viewer the feeling the artist had at the time the brush was set against the canvas. "If the picture was painted in the morning and you, as you look at the canvas, feel the cool shadows under the trees, the morning sun touching the mountain tops, and its light stealing in among the trees, and you feel as if the mists were yet lingering in the valleys, in fact, that is a beautiful morning, you have here a quality that is lasting."[7] Moore died in the Stone House in 1902.

Notes

INTRODUCTION

1. Hutton's work appeared in 1788 in the *Transactions of the Royal Society of Edinburgh*, followed by a multivolume version in 1795.

2. The Connecticut Valley rift is considered a failed rift because it did not evolve into a plate boundary. The large flood of basalt is called the central Atlantic magmatic province, or CAMP. Peter M. LeTourneau, *The Traprock Landscapes of New England: Environment, History, and Culture* (Middletown, CT: Wesleyan University Press, 2017), 45.

3. At least three of Percival's poems were reprinted in *McGuffey's Readers*. For the poetry that Dickinson read, see Jack L. Capps, *Emily Dickinson's Reading: 1836–1886* (Cambridge, MA: Harvard University Press, 1966). Harry R. Warfel, ed., *Uncollected Letters of James Gates Percival* (Gainesville, FL: University of Florida Press, 1959), v, xvii.

4. Jelle Zeilinga de Boer, *Stories in Stone: How Geology Influenced Connecticut History and Culture* (Middletown, CT: Wesleyan University Press, 2009), 16.

5. Robert Thorson, *Walden's Shore: Henry David Thoreau and Nineteenth-Century Science* (Boston: Harvard University Press, 2015), 271.

6. Julius H. Ward, *The Life and Letters of James Gates Percival* (Boston: Ticknor and Fields, 1866), 470.

7. Ibid., 469.

8. Ibid., 383–84.

9. Warfel, preface, v–vi.

1. A TRANQUIL AND TUMULTUOUS CHILDHOOD

1. Kensington was a parish in Berlin. Gates was the maiden name of Percival's grandmother. He used it to differentiate himself from his father. The Mattabesett River was called the Mill River.

2. James Gates Percival, *The Poetical Works of James Gates Percival*, 2 vols. (Boston: Ticknor and Fields, 1859). Both volumes are available online at HathiTrust.

3. The Connecticut Valley is a failed rift valley formed by the pulling apart of tectonic plates. There is uncertainty about the role of the traprock in the rerouting of the river. James D. Dana attributed the idea to Percival, although Percival himself did not explicitly say so in his geological report. Ward, 420–21. See also Michael Bell, *The Face of Connecticut: People, Geology and the Land*, State Geological and Natural History Survey of Connecticut (Hartford, CT: 1985), 126–27.

4. Ward, 4. Samuel Griswold Goodrich used the pen name Peter Parley. Samuel Griswold Goodrich, *Recollections of a Lifetime*, vol. 2 (New York: Miller, Orton, and Mulligan, 1856).

5. Emma Hart Willard was born in 1787. In a letter from Willard to Percival dated March 19, 1832, she explained how they were related and expressed her love for his father, who had been her physician. James Gates Percival Collection, YCAL MSS 703, Box 13, Folder 409, Series IV, Correspondence, Beinecke Rare Book & Manuscript Library. Alfred Andrews, *Genealogical History of Deacon Stephen Hart and His Descendants* (Hartford, CT: The Case, Lockwood & Brainard Co., 1875), 73–74.

6. Ward, 6.

7. Royal Robbins became minister of the Kensington Congregational Church in 1816. Ibid., 8–9. See also David Camp, *History of New Britain with Sketches of Farmington and Berlin Connecticut, 1640–1889* (New Britain, CT: William B. Thomson & Company, 1889), 252. Percival, *Poetical Works*, vol. 1, 60–61.

8. By the end of Percival's life, there were approximately 10,000 books in his library, of which 3,689 were auctioned off; among them was Goldsmith's *Natural History*. See *Catalogue of the valuable private library of the late James G. Percival* (Boston: Alfred Rudge & Son, 1860).

9. Morse was the father of Samuel F. B. Morse, who was an artist and the inventor of the telegraph. In *Universal Geography*, he speculated that because of the similarity in species found in the old and new worlds, there had once been only one continent that had shallow regions and

land bridges. Violent earthquakes forced subsidence and subsequent separation. Jedidiah Morse, *The American Universal Geography* (Boston: Isaiah Thomas and Ebenezer T. Andrews, 1793). Percival also read William Guthrie's *Geographical Historical and Commercial Grammar*. Ward, 395.

10. Ibid., 15, 18.

11. For more information on Peale's mammoth, see Richard Conniff, "Mammoths and Mastodons: All American Monsters," *Smithsonian Magazine*, April 2010.

12. Ward, 8.

13. During this period, the words mammoth and mastodon were used interchangeably. In his *Report on the Geology of the State of Connecticut*, Percival mentioned that a vertebra of a mammoth was found in a peat swamp in New Britain. In 1913, mastodon bones were unearthed in Farmington. Percival, *Report on the Geology of the State of Connecticut* (New Haven, CT: Osborn & Baldwin, 1842), 465. Percival, *Poetical Works*, vol. 1, 373.

14. Ward, 8.

15. Percival, *Poetical Works*, vol. 1, 62.

16. The "Commerciad" was 2,268 lines long. Curiously, William Cullen Bryant also wrote a satirical poem similar to the "Commerciad" when he was thirteen years old. Ward, 15.

17. James Gates Percival wrote some Masonic songs and may have been a member. His recollection of his father's medical skill is found in the poem "On My Father's Tomb." Percival, *Poetical Works*, vol. 2, 477.

18. Yale's medical school was established in 1810, but courses were not taught until 1813.

19. Horatio Gridley graduated from Yale in 1815 with Percival. The *Genealogical History of Deacon Stephen Hart and His Descendants* states that Dr. Percival died January 22, 1807, and that Harriet died February 16, 1807. Elizabeth fell ill in early February, at least six weeks after her initial exposure in December. Andrews, 73–74. Ward, 10–11.

20. Meningococcus was identified in 1887 by the Austrian bacteriologist Anton Weichselbaum. The analysis of Dr. Shirie C. Leng revealed that typhus syncopalis was probably meningococcemia caused by *Neisseria meningitidis*. Shirie C. Leng, MD, "Typhus Syncopalis: An Epidemic in Connecticut in 1823," *Connecticut Medicine* 76, no. 9 (October, 2012): 555–59.

21. Dr. Miner and his colleague Dr. Edward Cone saw approximately 360 people with the disease, of whom twelve died.

22. Goodrich, 338.

23. There is a reference in the genealogy of the Hart family to Oswin dying in a mental hospital. Andrews, 74. See also the reference to Oswin's insanity in Mark Langenfeld, "The Old Stonebreaker: James Gates Percival and the Lead Mines of Wisconsin," *Mining History Journal* (2012): 14. For Edwin, see Harry W. French, *Arts and Artists in Connecticut* (Boston: Lee and Shepard; New York: Charles T. Dillingham, 1879).

24. Ward, 33.

25. See Appendix I: Selected Poetry. In another version of the poem, Percival changed the word "deserted" to "haunted." Percival, *Poetical Works*, vol. 1, 58.

26. Percival left Long Island and returned to Kensington to study with several ministers in the area in preparation for Yale, among them Benoni Upson and Royal Robbins, Joab Brace in Newington, and Israel Woodward in Wolcott.

27. Ward, 38.

28. Percival, *Poetical Works*, vol. 1, 60.

2. BENJAMIN SILLIMAN BRINGS SCIENCE TO YALE

1. Silliman officially retired in 1849 but continued to teach until 1855.

2. Chandos Michael Brown, *Benjamin Silliman: A Life in the Young Republic* (Princeton: Princeton University Press, 1989), 55, 333n68.

3. Ibid., 57.

4. Ibid., 70, 334n24. See also George P. Merrill, *Contributions to the History of American Geology* (Washington, DC: Government Printing Office, 1906), 215.

5. Edgar F. Smith, *James Woodhouse, A Pioneer in Chemistry* (Philadelphia: The John C. Winston Company, 1918), 73.

6. Ibid., 74.

7. Silliman had to assent to the Westminster Confession and the Saybrook Platform, the constitution of the Congregational Church in Connecticut. He also made a statement of faith at the Yale chapel. Brown, 98, 105.

8. Ibid., 104–5, 109.

9. Maclean was professor of mathematics and natural philosophy at the College of New Jersey, which would be renamed Princeton. Ibid., 115.

10. Ibid., 116–18.

11. Merrill, 215.

12. It was one of Ussher's followers who came up with the exact date.

13. Percival also owned *The Principles of Moral and Political Philosophy* and *View of the Evidences of Christianity*.

14. Rachel Laudan, *From Mineralogy to Geology: The Foundations of a Science, 1650–1830* (Chicago: University of Chicago Press, 1987), 116.

15. Herbert Hovenkamp, *Science and Religion in America, 1800–1860* (Philadelphia: University of Pennsylvania Press, 1978), 123.

16. Laudan, 129.

17. Ibid., 115.

18. Ibid., 107.

19. Mott T. Greene, *Geology in the Nineteenth Century* (Ithaca and London: Cornell University Press, 1982), 35.

20. Werner rejected the idea that the water retreated into an abyss or caverns. Laudan, 93, 184.

21. Murray's *Comparative View of the Huttonian and Neptunian Systems of Geology* was published in 1802, the same year as Playfair's *Illustrations of the Huttonian Theory with Proofs and Illustrations*. Green, 48–50.

22. Hovenkamp, 123.

23. Merrill, 216.

24. The sketch was presented before the Connecticut Academy of Arts and Sciences, which subsequently published it. Merrill, 216; Brown, 203; Laudan, 117.

25. Brown, 203–5.

26. Ibid., 222.

27. Ibid., 225.

28. Percival, *Poetical Works*, vol. 1, 303–4.

29. Percival, "Curious Effect of Solar Light," *The American Journal of Science and Arts* 12 (1827): 164.

30. Goodrich, 356, 359.

31. William Chauncey Fowler, "James Gates Percival," *The Yale Literary Magazine* 27, no. 2 (November 1861): 56. Percival, *Poetical Works*, vol. 1, 28.

32. Ward, 34–35.

33. In the "Catalogue of the valuable private library of the late James G. Percival" (Boston: Alfred Rudge & Son, 1860), three books by Playfair are listed: *Geography and Statistical Description of Scotland*, *Outlines of Natural History*, and *Geometry*.

34. The location of the Percival portrait is unknown. Frederick Hull Cogswell, "James Gates Percival and His Friends," Connecticut Society

of the Order of the Founders and Patriots of America (New Haven: Tuttle, Morehouse & Taylor, 1902), 21.

35. Jelle Zeilinga De Boer and John Wareham, *New Haven Sentinels: The Art and Science of East Rock and West Rock* (Middletown, CT: Wesleyan University Press, 2013), 17.

3. PHYSICIAN, HEAL THYSELF

1. The voice problem had not kept Percival from performing in *Zamor*, a five-act play he had written. One friend claimed that Percival intentionally avoided being chosen valedictorian. Ward, 33–34, 36.

2. The handwritten speech does not have many punctuation marks. They have been added here for readability. YCAL MSS 703, Box 2, Folder 31, Series 1, Writings, 209. James Gates Percival Collection. Yale Collection of American Literature, Beinecke Rare Book and Manuscript Library.

3. Ibid.

4. Ward, 372.

5. Percival, *Poetical Works*, vol. 2, 213.

6. Ward, 47–48.

7. Ibid., 39.

8. Ibid., 44.

9. George Blumer, "Eli Ives—Practitioner, Teacher, Botanist," *Yale Journal of Biology and Medicine* (1932): 653.

10. Ibid., 652.

11. Ward, 78.

12. Blumer, 653.

13. Ibid, 653.

14. Ibid., 653. Ward, 48. Percival also translated from French *Physiological and chemical researches on the use of the prussic or hydro-cyanic acid in the treatment of diseases of the breast, and particularly in phthisis pulmonalis*, by F. Magendie, published by Howe & Spalding in New Haven in 1820.

15. Percival, *Poetical Works*, vol. 1, 100.

16. In an undated letter to Ives, Percival wrote, "A circumstance has arisen which induces me not to wish to be considered as engaged for the office. As you have not yet begun to fix it up, I hasten to give you this notice." Ward, 78. Blumer, 652.

17. Ward, 50.

18. Cornelius Tuthill, ed., *The Microscope* (New Haven: A. H. Maltby & Co., 1820), 196.

19. "The Suicide" has 132 stanzas of 4 lines each, for a total of 528 lines. Ward, 75.

20. Blumer, 662.

21. Ward, 57–58.

22. Catharine North, *History of Berlin Connecticut* (New Haven, CT: The Tuttle, Morehouse & Taylor Co., 1916), 216–18.

23. There were at least two outbreaks in 1823 and 1825. North lists Ward's death as 1823, while his headstone in the Ledge Cemetery and church records list it as 1825.

24. North, 219.

25. According to the Connecticut Church Record Abstracts, five children of Norman and Julia Winchell, aged three to five, died between August 25 and September 10, 1825. The family lived near the millpond, not far from the Percival home. Thanks to Sallie Caliandri of the Berlin Historical Society for this information.

26. Ward, 215.

27. Luke 4:23. Ward, 54.

28. See Appendix I: Selected Poetry; also Percival, *Poetical Works*, vol. 1, 282.

29. Percival had gone to Charleston with Charles Whitlow, a Scottish lecturer in horticulture who had a dubious reputation for herbal nostrums. They parted ways after their arrival. Caroline Gilman recalled that at his botanical lecture, Percival spoke in a whisper and got so flustered he crumbled up his notes and left the hall. YCAL MSS, 703 Box 18, Folder 441. James Gates Percival Collection. Yale Collection of American Literature, Beinecke Rare Book and Manuscript Library.

30. The letter is dated September 1822. Warfel, 6.

31. Ibid., xvi.

32. Ward, 292.

4. POETRY AS A WAY OF BEING

1. Warfel, 6.

2. Babcock & Son and Sidney's Press were located in New Haven, Sidney being the name of one of the sons. After Percival's return to New Haven, he lived in an apartment above Babcock's store.

3. Caroline Gilman's recollections were written many years later and are in the Beinecke Rare Book and Manuscript Library at Yale. She also wrote a humorous sketch of Percival delivering botanical and chemical lectures in the short story "Mr. Nible the Bashful Lecturer," published

in *Tales and Ballads &c* in 1839. YCAL MSS 703, Box 18, Folder 441. James Gates Percival Collection. Yale Collection of American Literature, Beinecke Rare Book and Manuscript Library.

4. See Appendix I: Selected Poetry; also *North American Review* 91, no. 188 (July 1860): 82.

5. *New York Mirror* 1, no. 9, September 27, 1823.

6. One critic later wrote, "Scientific exactness and scholarly accuracy appear continually in Percival's poetry, while his power of rendering language plastic as the potter's clay gives fullness to the expression and ease to the flow of his verse." *North American Review* 91: 85.

7. See Appendix I: Selection of Poetry. James Dwight Dana liked to quote "The Coral Grove" in his lectures on coral reef formation. "The Coral Grove" is still anthologized, most recently in *American Poetry: The Nineteenth Century, vol. 1: Freneau to Whitman* (1993), ed. John Hollander. It is also included in *Columbia Anthology of American Poetry* (1995), ed. Jay Parini.

8. Cogswell, 16.

9. The Gilmans owned house slaves. Letter to James Lawrence Yvonnet in Ward, 98.

10. Edward Robbins, *Historical Sketch of (Kensington) Berlin Conn During the Last One Hundred Years* (New Britain: Wm. A. House, 1876), 12.

11. See Appendix I: Selected Poetry for stanzas from "Prometheus."

12. Fowler, *Percival*, 58.

13. Percival's books are *Poems* (1821), *Clio I* (1822), *Clio II* (1822), *Prometheus II with Other Poems* (1822), *Poems* (1823), *Clio III* (1827), and *The Dream of a Day* (1843). He was also interested in history, delivering a speech before the Phi Beta Kappa Society at Yale on September 10, 1822, titled "On Some of the Moral and Political Truths Derivable From the Study of History."

14. An example is "The Mythology of Greece" in *Clio III.*

15. The title of the poem is "The Fragment." Percival, *Clio II*, preface, 6; *Clio III*, 76.

16. *North American Review* (January 1823). Warfel, 68. *New York Mirror* 5, no. 29, January 26, 1828.

17. Ward, 166, 171.

18. Ibid., 282.

19. The other five were Charles Sprague, John Pierpoint, Brooks (no first name), Edward Pinckney (also spelled Pinkney), and Washington Irving.

20. *Specimens of American Poetry* was edited by Samuel Kettell. *The Poets and Poetry of America* was edited by Rufus Griswold. Warfel, xvii.

21. During this period, Percival lived in Boston and Berlin, eventually settling in New Haven. Warfel, 10. Ward, 171. For the efforts of Cooper and Goodrich to publish his poetry, see Goodrich, 129–41.

22. Poe mentioned the name Percival in a note at the end of the story. According to Harry R. Warfel, Poe may have been referring to Dr. Thomas Percival, an English physician who wrote on medical ethics. See "Poe's 'Usher' Tarred & Fethered," referring to Poe's tale "The System of Dr. Tarr and Professor Fether," in *Marginalia*, published by the Edgar Allan Poe Society of Baltimore (online). See also Warfel, "Poe's Dr. Percival: A Note on the Fall of the House of Usher," *Modern Language Notes* 54, no. 2, February, 1939.

23. Percival is often compared to William Cullen Bryant (1794–1878), who was the influential editor of the *New York Evening Post*.

24. Ward, 74.

25. Percival sang Byron's praises in the introduction to his poem "Poetry."

26. Emma Willard attempted to get subscribers among students and teachers, writing to Percival "hearty good wishes" for success. James Gates Percival Collection, YCAL MSS 703, Box 13, Folder 409, Series IV, Correspondence, Beinecke Rare Book & Manuscript Library. *The New York Mirror* 9, no. 24, December 17, 1831.

27. Willis, 89. Goodrich, 141.

28. There was also a problem with his older brother, Edwin, who demanded money. An actor and an artist of moderate talent, Edwin was creative and unstable.

29. Ward, 387; Althea Green, "The James Gates Percival Papers," *The Yale University Library Gazette* 28, no. 2 (New Haven, CT: Yale University Press, October 1953): 79. See also Joshua Kendall, *The Forgotten Founding Father: Noah Webster's Obsession and the Creation of American Culture* (New York: G. P. Putnam's Son, 2011).

30. See Appendix I: Selected Poetry. Percival, *Poetical Works*, vol. 1, xxxiv.

31. Cole painted Prometheus lit by a strong western sun. See Rebecca Bedell, *The Anatomy of Nature: Geology & American Landscape Painting, 1825–1875* (Princeton and Oxford: Princeton University Press, 2001), 32–33.

32. Leo Marx, *The Machine in the Garden: Technology and the Pastoral Ideal in America* (New York: Oxford University Press, 1964), 4, 26, 164, 375.

33. The lecture was delivered in 1837. Ralph Waldo Emerson, *Essays and Poems by Ralph Waldo Emerson* (New York: Barnes & Noble Classics, 2004), 64.

34. Goodrich, 141.

5. THE SHIFT TO GEOLOGY

1. Percival, *Poetical Works*, vol. 1, 489.

2. There are two poems, "To Seneca Lake" and "Seneca Lake." Percival also went to the Catskill Mountains in 1818 and New Jersey in 1828 to study the Palisades and the Watchung Mountains.

3. Percival, "Dr. Van Rensselaer on Salt," *The American Journal of Science and Arts* 7 (1824): 360–62. See also Ward, 107.

4. Ward included "The Philosopher" in the appendix of the biography. It was published in *The Knickerbocker New-York Magazine* in 1836. Ward, 533.

5. Brongniart's *Treatise on the Classification and Distribution of the Fossil Vegetables* was reviewed by Percival in the *American Journal of Science and Arts* 7:170–85. Other articles were on the zoological characters of formations, curious effect of solar light, and the hematite of Connecticut.

6. Also called *Précis of World Geography*.

7. It carried a notation on the title page: "with additions and corrections by James G. Percival." Warfel, 69.

8. Although Percival did not know it, the Deccan traps were caused by volcanic eruptions far larger than the ones that created some of the Connecticut trap. *American Journal of Science and Arts* 7: 361.

9. Percival Papers, YCAL, MSS 703, Clippings General (1 of 2 folders), March 18, 1823, Beinecke Rare Book and Manuscript Library.

10. Percival, *American Journal of Science and Arts* 5(1822): 42.

11. Edward Robbins, *Historical Sketch of (Kensington) Berlin* (New Britain, CT: Wm. A. House, 1876), 11.

12. Greene, 78.

13. For an analysis of Silliman's views, see Hovenkamp, 125–29.

14. Lyell's ideas had less impact in Europe, where geologists were focused more on the nature of mountain building. Laudan, 202.

15. Greene, 70–71.

16. Charles Lyell, *Journal of a Tour in North America* (London: John Murray, 1845), 13.

17. In 1836, Silliman wrote to Lyell that *Principles* was being reprinted in Philadelphia. Katharine Murray Lyell, ed., *Life, Letters and Journals of Sir Charles Lyell* (London: John Murray, 1881), 471.

18. Laudan, 218.

19. Hitchcock (1793–1864) eventually became president of Amherst College and president of the American Association for the Advancement of Science. He also identified the 150-mile-long glacial lake that filled much of the Connecticut Valley at the end of the last ice age. The lake was named after him.

20. Other state surveys were conducted in 1836 in Maine, New York, Ohio, and Pennsylvania; in 1837 in Delaware, Indiana, Michigan; and in 1839 in New Hampshire and Rhode Island. Edward Hitchcock, *Sketch of the Scenery of Massachusetts* (Northampton: J. H. Butler, 1842), iv.

21. J. J. Stevenson, "Presidential Address," *The Geological Society Bulletin* 10 (December 1898): 83–98. For the Rogers brothers, see Sean Patrick Adams, "Partners in Geology, Brothers in Frustration: The Antebellum Surveys of Virginia and Pennsylvania," *The Virginia Magazine of History and Biography* 106 (Winter 1998): 5–34.

6. THE CONNECTICUT GEOLOGICAL SURVEY

1. Charles Upham Shepard, *Report on the Geological Survey of Connecticut* (New Haven, CT: S. L. Hamlen, 1837), 10.

2. Ibid.

3. Silliman claimed he recommended Percival to the governor.

4. James Gates Percival, *Report on the Geology of the State of Connecticut* (New Haven, CT: Osborn & Baldwin, 1842), 367.

5. Following the Civil War, people thought the stone face looked like Lincoln.

6. John Warner Barber, *Connecticut Historical Collections* (New Haven: John W. Barber, 1836).

7. Ward, 390–91.

8. Ibid., 394–95.

9. Ibid., 388–89.

10. Ibid., 401.

11. Shepard, 8.

12. Ward, 354, 362, 383–84, 477.

13. Richard S. Willis made his comment in a biographical sketch in *Poetical Works of James Gates Percival*, vol. 1, xxvii. Warfel, 41.

14. Ward, 353.

15. There is no evidence that Percival had read Agassiz's book by the time the Connecticut report was published. Percival mentioned visiting Dobson's factory in Vernon in the report. Percival, *Report*, 181, 465. See also Bell, *Face of Connecticut*, 123.

16. Percival, *Report*, 181.

17. Ibid., 35.

18. Ward, 370.

19. Percival, *Report*, 297. Ward, 370.

20. Percival, *Report*, 11.

21. Percival asked many questions that he could not possibly answer, such as the reason for the curvilinear form of some of the ridges. He and James Dana contemplated erroneously the idea of a cooling and contracting earth in which the withdrawal of heat would tend to create curvilinear forms as the lava hardened. James D. Dana, "Origin of the Grand Outline Features of the Earth," *American Journal of Science and Arts* (May, 1847): 381–83.

22. Warfel, 45.

23. De Boer, *Stories in Stone*, 16.

24. Ward, 403–4.

25. Dana, 381.

26. Ward, 372.

7. AN INTERMEZZO OF MUSIC AND LANGUAGE

1. Percival's rock collection and library may have been in the same room, with his bedroom in the second and living area in the third. The few people who glimpsed the apartment remarked that it was a mess. Ward, 364, 463.

2. Adolph B. Benson, "James Gates Percival, Student of German Culture," *The New England Quarterly* 2, no. 4 (October 1929): 606.

3. Ibid., 609.

4. Percival wrote in a letter, "Goethe and Schiller rule my soul, but not like Shakespeare and Milton." Warfel, 71.

5. On June 4, 1832, Percival wrote to Ticknor about the narrative poem *Der arme Heinrich*, composed at the end of the twelfth century in Middle High German that Percival was translating. Benson, 611. Ward, 426–31.

6. The biographical sketch is in the preface to *The Poetical Works of James Gates Percival*, vol. 1, xxxvii.

7. Ibid., 609. Ward, 423.

8. Arthur P. Coleman, "Talvj's Correspondence with James Gates Percival," *The Slavonic and East European Review: American Series* 3, no. 3 (October 1944): 88, 95.

9. Ibid., 96.

10. Ward, 400.

11. Benson, 607.

12. Ward, 441.

13. This was not the only time that a dirge by Percival was sung in public. Following his death, Percival's poem "Oh! It is Great for Our Country to Die" was set to music by Alfred Delaney and was sung by a choir after the delivery of the Gettysburg Address by Abraham Lincoln on November 19, 1863. Ibid., 444.

14. Richard S. Willis was a musician and composer. He was the brother of Nathaniel Parker Willis and Fanny Fern. Ibid., 437.

15. Ibid., 424.

16. Ibid., 378, 463.

17. During the 1830s, Percival published several poems in *Knickerbocker* and other publications. Percival, *The Dream of a Day*, preface, iv–v.

18. Ralph Waldo Emerson, "The Dream of a Day," *Dial Essays*, 1843. See also Ward, 458.

19. Dr. George Hayward, chair of surgery at Harvard, had befriended Percival in the 1820s, helping him get editorial contracts. Charles Hayward had graduated from Harvard with Thoreau and had joined him on early adventures, including staying at a shanty built by Charles Wheeler, which was the precursor to the cabin at Walden.

20. It is possible that the description of the visitor is a composite of Alcott and Percival. Self-educated, Alcott was born in 1799 in Wolcott, Connecticut. Percival was never a peddler, but he did indeed peddle his poetry. In his journal entry of May 9, 1853, written six years after the visitor came to Walden, Thoreau described spending that spring day with Alcott. In preparing the final draft of *Walden*, published the following year in 1854, Thoreau incorporated some of the journal entry but, curiously, not all. Henry David Thoreau, *Walden, or Life in the Woods* (New York: Fall River Press, 2017), 234–35. Bradford Torrey and Francis H. Allen, eds., *The Journal of Henry D. Thoreau, March 5, 1853–November 30, 1853* (Boston: Houghton Mifflin, 1949), 130–31.

8. WEST TO THE FRONTIER OF WISCONSIN

1. Ward, 477–78.

2. J. G. Percival and C. T. Jackson, "Reports on the Albert Coal Mines," *American Journal of Science and Arts*, 2nd ser., 13 (1852): 276. Ward, 475.

3. Ward used the initials F. C. for Phelps, but an American Mining Company stock certificate bears the initials F. E. The stock certificate shows that the company was incorporated in Vermont in 1849. Mark Langenfeld, "The Old Stonebreaker: James Gates Percival and the Lead Mines of Wisconsin," *Mining History Journal* 19 (2012): 7.

4. In his essay "Walking," as well in other works, Thoreau expressed his desire to go west, which he achieved briefly from May to July 1861. He died May 6, 1862.

5. *History of Grant County*, 6–7.

6. Joseph Schafer, *The Wisconsin Lead Region*, (Madison: State Historical Society of Wisconsin, 1932), 96.

7. Ibid., 7.

8. The letter is dated August 1, 1853. Herrick served as Percival's financial advisor. Ward, 472–73, 482.

9. Presumably Percival read the poem in English to his friends. *History of Grant County*, 11.

10. Ibid., 10. See William H. Pearson, "James Gates Percival," 145, quoting from H. D. York in the *Grant County Advocate*. See also Jonathan Henry Evans, "Some Reminiscences of Early Grant County," *Proceedings of the State Historical Society of Wisconsin* (1909), 232–72.

11. *History of Grant County*, 10.

12. Ward, 486.

13. Ibid., 482. See also "Journal of Silver and Lead Mining Operations: Operations of the American Mining Company in Wisconsin," *Mining Magazine* 2 (1854): 691.

14. Ward, 481. *History of Grant County*, 11.

15. The first survey of Wisconsin, Iowa, and the northern part of Illinois was done in 1840 by David Dale Owen, a geologist who worked under the direction of the General Land Office. Merrill, 353.

16. Warfel, xix.

17. Ibid., 65.

18. Percival's speculations about drift current were wrong. The ice sheet did not cover the southwest region of Wisconsin.

19. James G. Percival, *Annual Report on the Geological Survey of the State of Wisconsin*, (Madison, WI: Beriah Brown, 1855), 10.

20. "Poet and First State Geologist," *Grant County News*, February 1918.

21. Winnebago is related to the Siouan language group, and Chippewa is related to the Algonquian language group. Ward, 512.

22. Warfel, 144.

23. Ward, 509–10. Benson, "James Gates Percival," 604.

24. A preemptioner held a right to purchase certain public lands. Warfel, 65–66.

25. Ward, 500.

26. Ibid., 501, 505.

27. Italics in original. Ibid., 504.

28. Ibid., 493.

29. Ibid., 512. Percival, *Wisconsin Report*, 7, 21, 101.

30. Percival, *Wisconsin Report*, 32, 91.

31. Ibid., 96.

32. Ward, 490.

33. Warfel, 66–67.

34. Ibid., 67.

35. *History of Grant County*, 11.

36. A strange story that circulated after Percival's death indicated that he thought he had rabies, having been bitten by a dog, which was subsequently found to be healthy. Supposedly Dr. Jenckes tried to reassure him, but Percival refused to take any liquids. Yet the letters of Jenckes, who was Percival's executor, do not bear out the story. Jenckes noted that Percival consumed coffee in large quantities toward the end of his life, which ties back both to Percival's research with Dr. Eli Ives in 1818 and with his taking copious quantities of coffee following his opium overdose. Newspaper articles from the time of his death mention Percival's depression and that his "disease was no doubt heightened by a most sensitive fancy." Langenfeld, "The Old Stonebreaker," 14–15. Ward, 512–13.

EPILOGUE

1. Goodrich, 129.

2. Ward, 461.

3. Lowell's review was of Ward's biography. See James Russell Lowell, "The Life and Letters of James Gates Percival," in *Letters of James Russell Lowell*, vol. 2 (Harper Brothers, 1894).

4. John Hay, "The Limits of Recovery: The Failure of James Gates Percival," *Early American Literature* 55, no. 1 (2020): 115, 127.

5. Greene, 292.

6. LeTourneau, *Traprock Landscapes*, 57, 60.

APPENDIX 2. THE ART OF NELSON AUGUSTUS MOORE

1. For more information on Moore, see Ellen Fletcher, *Nelson Augustus Moore* (Moore Family Trust, 1994); Nelson Augustus Moore, *Autobiography*, manuscripts, Connecticut State Library Digital Collections; Ethelbert Moore, *The Tenth Generation*, published privately.

2. Moore, *Autobiography*, 3.

3. Moore, *The Tenth Generation*, 15.

4. Moore, *Autobiography*. Rebecca Bedell, *The Anatomy of Nature: Geology & American Landscape Painting 1825–1875* (Princeton: Princeton University Press, 2001), 51.

5. Fletcher, *Moore*, 35.

6. Ibid., 54.

7. Ibid., 58.

Bibliography

Adams, Sean Patrick. "Partners in Geology, Brothers in Frustration: The Antebellum Geological Surveys of Virginia and Pennsylvania." *The Virginia Magazine of History and Biography* 106, no. 1 (Winter 1998): 5–34.

Andrews, Alfred. *Genealogical History of Deacon Stephen Hart and his Descendants: 1632–1875*. Hartford, CT: The Case, Lockwood & Brainard Co., 1875.

Barber, John Warner. *Connecticut Historical Collections*. New Haven, CT: John W. Barber; Hartford, CT: A. Willard, 1836.

Bedell, Rebecca. *The Anatomy of Nature: Geology & American Landscape Painting, 1825–1875*. Princeton and Oxford: Princeton University Press, 2001.

Bell, Michael. *The Face of Connecticut: People, Geology and the Land*. Bulletin 110, State Geological and Natural History Survey of Connecticut, 1985.

Benson, Adolph B. "James Gates Percival Student of German Culture." *The New England Quarterly* 2, no. 4 (October 1929): 603–624.

Bickford, Christopher P. and J. Bard McNulty, eds. *John Warner Barber's Views of Connecticut Towns, 1834–36*. The Acorn Club and The Connecticut Historical Society, 1990.

Blake, James Kingsley. "The Microscope and James Gates Percival." *Papers of the New Haven Colony Historical Society* 8. New Haven: Tuttle, Morehouse & Taylor Press, 1914.

Blumer, George. "Eli Ives—Practitioner, Teacher, Botanist." *Yale Journal of Biology and Medicine* 4 (May 1932): 649–63.

Brown, Chandos Michael. *Benjamin Silliman: A Life in the Young Republic*. Princeton: Princeton University Press, 1989.

Caliandri, Sarah, and Cathy Nelson. "James Gates Percival, 1795–1856." Berlin, CT: Berlin Historical Society, unpublished manuscript.

Camp, David. *History of New Britain with Sketches of Farmington and Berlin Connecticut, 1640–1889*. New Britain, CT: William B. Thomson & Company, 1889.

Capps, Jack L. *Emily Dickinson's Reading: 1836–1886*. Cambridge, MA: Harvard University Press, 1966.

Catalogue of the valuable private library of the late James G. Percival, Leonard & Co. Auctioneers. Boston: Alfred Rudge & Son, 1860.

Cogswell, Frederick Hull. "James Gates Percival and His Friends: An Address at a Meeting of the Connecticut Society of the Order of the Founders and Patriots of America, April 19, A.D. 1902." New Haven, CT: The Tuttle, Morehouse & Taylor Company.

Coleman, Arthur P. "Talvj's Correspondence with James Gates Percival." *The Slavonic and East European Review. American Series* 3, no. 3. (October, 1944): 83–96.

Conniff, Richard. "Mammoths and Mastodons: All American Monsters." *Smithsonian Magazine*, April 2010.

De Boer, Jelle Zeilinga. *Stories in Stone: How Geology Influenced Connecticut History and Culture*. Middletown, CT: Wesleyan University Press, 2009.

De Boer, Jelle Zeilinga, and John Wareham. *New Haven's Sentinels: The Art and Science of East Rock and West Rock*. Middletown, CT: Wesleyan University Press, 2013.

Dillman, Richard, ed. *The Major Essays of Henry David Thoreau*. Albany: Whitston Publishing Company, Inc., 2001.

Emerson, Ralph Waldo. "The Dream of a Day." *The Dial*, April 1843.

Evans, Jonathan Henry. "Some Reminiscences of Early Grant County." *Proceedings of the State Historical Society of Wisconsin* (1909): 232–72.

Fisher, George P. *Life of Benjamin Silliman*. 2 vols. Philadelphia: Porter & Coates, 1866; New York: Charles Scribner and Co., 1866.

Fletcher, Ellen. *Nelson Augustus Moore*. Moore Picture Trust and Northeastern University Press, 1994.

"Forgotten Poet: A Strange Life." *Chicago Tribune*, October 24, 1895. www.wisconsinhistory.org/Records/Newspaper/BA2450.

Fowler, William Chauncey. "James Gates Percival." *The Yale Literary Magazine* 27, no. 2 (November 1861): 53–60.

French, Harry Willard. *Arts and Artists in Connecticut*. Boston: Lee and Shepard; New York: Charles T. Dillingham, 1879.

Gilman, Caroline. *Tales and Ballads &c.* New York: Samuel Colman, 1839.

Gilman, Daniel C. *The Life of James Dwight Dana.* New York and London: Harper & Brothers, 1899.

Goodrich, Samuel Griswold. *Recollections of a Lifetime.* Vol. 2. New York: Miller, Orton, and Mulligan, 1856.

Greene, Mott T. *Geology in the Nineteenth Century: Changing Views of a Changing World.* Ithaca and London: Cornell University Press, 1982.

Griswold, Rufus Wilmot. *The Poets and Poetry of America: To the Middle of the Nineteenth Century.* Philadelphia: Parry and McMillan, 1851.

Hay, John. "The Limits of Recovery: The Failure of James Gates Percival." *Early American Literature* 55, no. 1 (2020): 111–44.

History of Grant County Wisconsin, 1881. genealogytrails.com/wis/grant /hazelgreen.html.

Hitchcock, Edward. *Elementary Geology.* New York: M. H. Newman & Co., 1847.

———. *Sketch of the Scenery of Massachusetts.* Northampton: J. H. Butler, 1842.

Hovenkamp, Herbert. *Science and Religion in America, 1800–1860.* Philadelphia: University of Pennsylvania Press, 1978.

"James Gates Percival." *New York Mirror,* September 24, 1825; January 26, 1828; July 3, 1830.

"James Gates Percival: Poet, Geologist, Musician and Linguist," *Milwaukee Sentinel,* July 27, 1897. www.wisconsinhistory.org/Records /Newspaper/BA208.

"Journal of Silver and Lead Mining Operations: Operations of the American Mining Company in Wisconsin," *Mining Magazine* 2 (1854): 691.

Kendall, Joshua. *The Forgotten Founding Father: Noah Webster's Obsession and the Creation of American Culture.* New York: G. P. Putnam's Son, 2011.

Langenfeld, Mark. "The 'Old Stonebreaker': James Gates Percival and the Lead Mines of Wisconsin." *Mining History Journal* 19 (2012): 1–18. www.mininghistoryassociation.org/Journal/MHJ-v19-2012-Langen feld.pdf.

Laudan, Rachel. *From Mineralogy to Geology: The Foundations of a Science, 1650–1830.* Chicago: University of Chicago Press, 1987.

Leng, Shirie C. "Typhus Syncopalis: An Epidemic in Connecticut in 1823." *Connecticut Medicine* 76, no. 9 (October 2012): 555–59.

LeTourneau, Peter M. *The Traprock Landscapes of New England: Environment, History and Culture.* Photography by Robert Pagini. Middletown, CT: Wesleyan University Press, 2017.

Lowell, James Russell. *The Complete Works of James Russell Lowell.* Boston: Houghton Mifflin, 1898.

Lyell, Katharine Murray Lyell, ed. *Life, Letters and Journals of Sir Charles Lyell.* London: John Murray, 1881.

Malte-Brun, M. *A System of Universal Geography or a Description of All the Parts of the World.* Vols. 1–3. Edited by James G. Percival. Boston: Samuel Walker, 1834; Babel:hathitrust.org.

Marx, Leo. *The Machine in the Garden: Technology and the Pastoral Ideal in America.* Oxford: Oxford University Press, 1964, 2000.

Merrill, George P. *Contributions to the History of American Geology.* Washington: Government Printing Office, 1906.

Micklethwait, David. *Noah Webster and the American Dictionary.* Jefferson, NC: MarFarland & Co, 2000.

Milici, Robert C. and C. R. Bruce Hobbs Jr. "William Barton Rogers and the First Geological Survey of Virginia, 1835–1841." *Earth Sciences History* 6, no. 1 (1987): 3–13.

Moore, Ethelbert Allen. *The Tenth Generation.* Private publication, 1950.

Morse, Edward Lind. *Samuel F. B. Morse: His Letters and Journals.* Boston: Houghton Mifflin, 1914.

Morse, Jedidiah. *The American Universal Geography or a View of the Present State of the Empires, Kingdoms, States and Republics in the Known World and of the United States of America in Particular in Two Parts.* Boston: Isaiah Thomas and Ebenezer T. Andrews, 1793.

Mowry, Duane. "James Gates Percival." *Lancaster Teller,* October 15, 1903. www.wisconsinhistory.org/Records/Newspaper/BA2455.

North, Catharine. *History of Berlin Connecticut.* New Haven, CT: The Tuttle, Morehouse & Taylor Co., 1916.

Pearson, William H. "James Gates Percival." *The Wisconsin Magazine of History* 9, no. 2 (December 1924): 131–45.

Peck, S. A. "Anecdotes of Olden Time." *The Church Record, Kensington Congregational Church* 5, no. 6 (May 1890): 1.

Percival, James Gates. *Clio I.* Charleston, SC: Babcock, 1822.

———. *Clio II.* New Haven, CT: S. Converse, 1822.

———. *Clio III.* New York: G. and C. Carvill, 1827.

———. *The Dream of a Day and Other Poems.* New Haven, CT: S. Babcock, 1843.

———. "Life: An Allegory," *Knickerbocker* 7 (January 1836): 48.

———. *Poems.* New Haven, CT: A. H. Maltby & Co., Printers, 1821.

———. *Poems.* New York: Charles Wiley, 1823.

———. *Poetical Works of James Gates Percival.* 2 vols. Boston: Ticknor and Fields, 1859.

———. *Report on the Geological Survey of the State of Wisconsin.* Madison: Beriah Brown, 1855.

———. *Report on the Geology of the State of Connecticut.* New Haven, CT: Osborn & Baldwin, 1842.

———. *Report on the iron of Dodge and Washington counties, State of Wisconsin.* Milwaukee: Starrs' Book and Job Printing Office, 1855.

Pettee, J. T. "James G. Percival, M. D." *Transactions of Meriden Scientific Association* 4 (1889–1890): 22–38.

"Poet and First State Geologist," *Grant County News*, February 1918. www.wisconsinhistory.org/Records/Newspaper/BA2484.

Pratt, Rev. Magee. "James Gates Percival, Poet and Scientist." *The Connecticut Magazine*, February 1900, 81–85.

Robbins, Edward W. *Historical Sketch of (Kensington) Berlin Conn During the Last One Hundred Years.* New Britain, CT: Wm. A. House, 1876.

Schafer, Joseph. *The Wisconsin Lead Region.* Madison: State Historical Society of Wisconsin, 1932.

Shepard, Charles Upham. *Report on the Geological Survey of Connecticut.* New Haven, CT: S. L. Hamlen, 1837.

Silliman, Benjamin. "Igneous origin of some traprocks." *American Journal of Science and Arts* 17 (1830): 119–32.

Smith, Edgar F. *James Woodhouse, A Pioneer in Chemistry, 1770–1809.* Philadelphia: John C. Winston Company, 1918.

Smith, Herbert F. "Is Roderick Usher a Caricature?" *Poe Studies* 6, no. 2 (December 1973): 49–50.

Thoreau, Henry David. *The Correspondence. Vol. 1: 1834–1848.* Edited by Robert N. Hudspeth. Princeton: Princeton University Press, 2013.

———. *The Correspondence, Vol. 2: 1849–1856.* Edited by Robert N. Hudspeth, Elizabeth Hall Witherell, and Lihong Xie. Princeton: Princeton University Press, 2018.

———. *Journal. Vol. 2: 1842–1848.* General Editor, John C. Broderick. Edited by Robert Sattelmeyer. Princeton: Princeton University Press, 1984.

———. *Journal, March 5, 1853–November 30, 1853*. Edited by Bradford Torrey and Francis H. Allen. Boston: Houghton Mifflin, 1949.

———. *Walden, or Life in the Woods*. New York: Fall River Press, 2017.

Thorson, Robert. *Walden's Shore: Henry David Thoreau and Nineteenth-Century Science*. Boston: Harvard University Press, 2015.

Walls, Laura Dassow. *Henry David Thoreau*. Chicago: University of Chicago Press, 2017.

Ward, Julius, H. *The Life and Letters of James Gates Percival*. Boston: Ticknor and Fields, 1866.

Warfel, Harry R., ed. *Uncollected Letters of James Gates Percival, Poet and Geologist, 1795–1856*. University of Florida Monographs, Humanities, No. 1. Gainesville, FL: University of Florida Press, 1959.

Willis, Nathaniel Parker. "James Gates Percival, The Editor's Table." *American Monthly Magazine*, July 1830, 286–89.

Wilson, Althea Green. "The James Gates Percival Papers." *The Yale University Library Gazette* 28, no. 2 (October 1953): 77–81.

Wright, C. A. "James Gates Percival, Poet and Scientist." *Connecticut Magazine* 7, no. 2 (1900): 87–92.

Index

Garnet Books

Titles with asterisks (*) are also in the Driftless Connecticut Series

About the Author

Kathleen L. Housley is the author of eleven books. Her poems and essays on science and the humanities have appeared in many national publications, including *Image*, *Terra Nova* (MIT Press), *The Christian Century*, and the online journals *Biologos* and *Metanexus*. In the field of materials science, Housley is the author of *Black Sand: The History of Titanium* and she has served as an editor of scientific publications. Her previous book is *The Scientific World of Karl-Friedrich Bonhoeffer: The Entanglement of Science, Religion, and Politics in Nazi Germany* (Palgrave Macmillan, 2019). She has taught courses on the interconnections between the sciences, humanities, and art at the Academy of Lifelong Learning, Trinity College, in Hartford, Connecticut.

About the Driftless Connecticut Series

The Driftless Connecticut Series is a publication award program established in 2010 to recognize excellent books with a Connecticut focus or written by a Connecticut author. To be eligible, the book must have a Connecticut topic or setting or an author must have been born in Connecticut or have been a legal resident of Connecticut for at least three years.

The Driftless Connecticut Series is funded by the Beatrice Fox Auerbach Foundation Fund at the Hartford Foundation for Public Giving.

For more information and a complete list of books in the Driftless Connecticut Series, please visit us online at weslpress.org /driftless.